SKILL SHARPENERS
Science
2

Contents

Physical Science

Life Science

Space and Earth Science

Earth's Systems

Science and Engineering

Skill Sharpeners—Science • EMC 5322 • © Evan-Moor Corp.

Solid, Liquid, Gas

Look at the picture. Read the word.
Write the word in the sentence.

solid

A _____ has its own shape and does not flow.

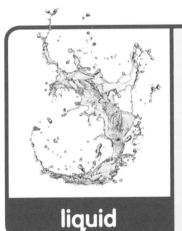

liquid

A _____ flows but does not have its own shape.

gas

A _____ does not have its own shape and is invisible.

Physical Science

Matter

Solid, Liquid, Gas

Everything around us is called matter.
Matter is anything that takes up space.

Matter has three forms:
solid, **liquid**, and **gas**.

liquid

gas

solid

Matter

A **solid** has its own shape. A solid will not change unless you do something to it, like cut it or melt it.

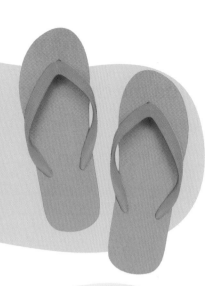

A **liquid** does not have its own shape. A liquid can flow, drip, and splash. It will take the shape of what it is in.

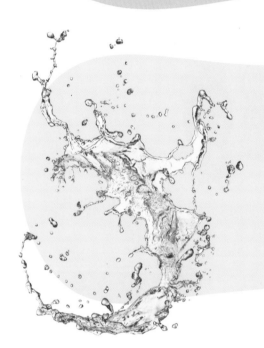

A **gas** is invisible. Air is made of gases. You cannot see air, but you can see what air does.

Matter

Skill:

Apply science vocabulary in context

Word Play

Read the clue. Write the word.

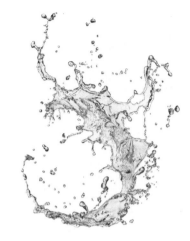

1. A liquid can

   f __ __ __.
   ₁

2. It has its own shape.

   __ __ __ __ __

3. It is made of gases.

   __ __ __
   2   5

4. It has three forms.

   __ __ __ __ __
       3   4

Write the numbered letters to solve the puzzle.

Science Puzzle

__ __ __ __ __ is a liquid.
1   2   3   4   5

Matter

10

Sorting Matter Chart

Skill:
Complete charts or graphs to categorize information

Write each word in the chart.

milk	rock	water	air	toy

solid	liquid	gas

Physical Science

Matter

11

Three Balloons

Skill:
Conduct experiments and record results

What You Need

- 3 balloons of different colors
- water

What You Do

1. Fill one balloon halfway with water. Freeze overnight. The next day, take out the frozen balloon. This is your solid balloon. How does it feel? Write it on the next page.

2. Fill another balloon halfway with water. This is your liquid balloon. How does it feel? Write it on the next page.

3. Blow up another balloon. This is your gas balloon. How does it feel? Write it on the next page.

4. Toss each balloon. Write what happened on the next page.

Physical Science

Write what happened when you tossed the balloons.

What Happened?

Frozen

How did it feel? _____

What happened when I tossed it?

_____

Liquid

How did it feel? _____

What happened when I tossed it?

_____

Gas

How did it feel? _____

What happened when I tossed it?

_____

Matter

Matter Chart

Solids, liquids, and gases are kinds of matter. Complete the chart to show how they are alike or different.

Matter	Does it have its own shape?	Can you see it?	Write one example.
solid			
liquid			
gas			

Melting, Freezing, Mixing

Look at the picture. Read the word.
Write the word in the sentence.

melt

When you _____ something, it goes from a solid to a liquid.

freeze

When you _____ something, it goes from a liquid to a solid.

mixture

When you put different things together, you make a _____.

Concept:

Matter can change when it is mixed, heated, or cooled.

changes in Matter

Melting, Freezing, and Mixing

Matter can change in different ways.

It can change from a solid to a liquid.

It can change from a liquid to a solid.

Heat can change matter. The heat from the stove changed this butter. The butter changed from solid to liquid. The butter **melted**.

Cold air can change matter. Cold air will **freeze** water. The water changed from a liquid to a solid. The water froze and became ice cubes.

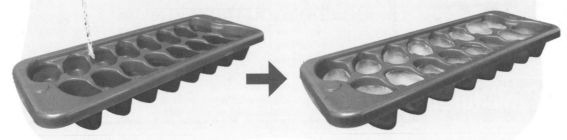

Another thing you can do with matter is mix it. You can put together different things and make a mixture.

a mixture of fruit

Things that make up a mixture do not change when you put them together.

This mixture has many different kinds of fruit. If you take a cherry out of the mixture, the cherry keeps the same shape that it had when it was in the mixture.

Word Play

Read the clue. Write the word.

1. Solid to liquid

   —— —— —— ——
         5   1

2. Liquid to solid

   —— —— —— —— —— —— ——
      2

3. Two or more things mixed together

   —— —— —— —— —— —— ——
   6   4   7

4. To become different

   —— —— —— —— —— ——
            3

Use the numbered letters to solve the puzzle.

Science Puzzle

—— —— —— —— —— —— —— ——
1   2   3   4   5   6   4   7

is a kind of mixture.

Changes in Matter

Look at the diagrams.

heating

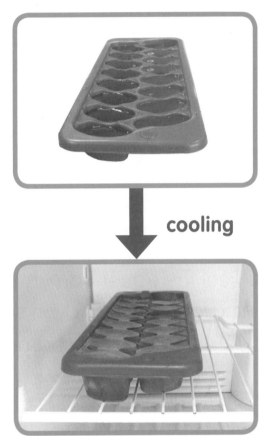

cooling

In what way did the butter change?

_____

_____

_____

_____

In what way did the water change?

_____

_____

_____

_____

Changes in Matter

Physical Science

changes in Matter

Crayon Paperweight

What You Need

- crayons
- 2 smooth flat stones
- 2 paper plates

What You Do

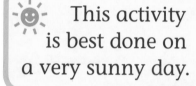

☼ This activity is best done on a very sunny day.

1. Peel the paper from the crayons. Make crayon shavings by using a pencil sharpener.

2. Place each stone on a paper plate. Sprinkle crayon shavings on top of each stone.

3. Set one crayon-covered stone in direct sunlight. Set the other crayon-covered stone in the shade.

4. After one hour, check the stones. What happened? Write or draw to tell about any changes.

Stone 1

What I did: _____

What happened: _____

_____

What it looks like:

Stone 2

What I did: _____

What happened: _____

_____

What it looks like:

Physical Science

Changes in Matter

Skill:

Write sentences to demonstrate understanding of science concepts

Changes in Matter

Changes Chart

Write a sentence about each picture.

_____

_____

_____

_____

_____

_____

Force Makes Things Move

Look at the picture. Read the word.
Write the word in the sentence.

push

When you _____ something, you move it away from you.

pull

When you _____ something, you bring it closer to you.

force

A _____ is something that makes an object move.

x

Forces and Motion

Concept:

Pushing and pulling can change the position and motion of objects.

Forces and Motion

Force Makes Things Move

Think of how you make things move. You can use your hands or your body to move something.

You can **push** something away from you.

You can **pull** something toward you.

A push or a pull is called a **force**. A force makes something move. A force also stops something from moving.

You use more force to push or pull heavier things.

You use less force to push or pull lighter things.

Forces and Motion

What Kind of Force?

Look at the picture. What kind of force is it?
Write either **pull** or **push**.

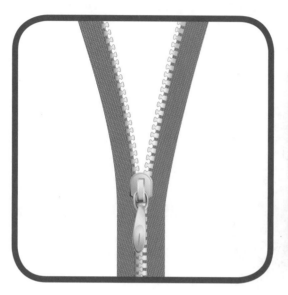

_____

_____

_____

_____

Push, Pull, or Both?

Skill:

Interpret information from graphic images

Read the diagram.

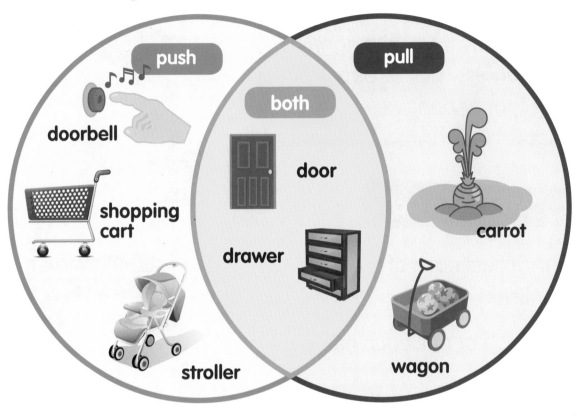

push

pull

both

doorbell

door

shopping cart

carrot

drawer

stroller

wagon

Forces and Motion

1. What is an object that moves with a push?

_____

2. What is an object that moves with a pull?

_____

3. What is an object that moves with both a push and a pull?

_____

Physical Science   **27**

Forces and Motion

The Force of a Push or Pull

What You Need

- chair
- book
- pot or pan
- wagon
- paper clip

What You Do

1. Collect each of the items listed above.

2. Push or pull each item.

3. Write about what you did and what happened in the chart on the next page.

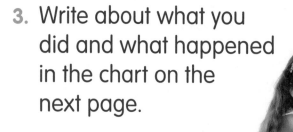

Item	Pushed or Pulled	What happened? Did you have to use a lot of force?
toy	pushed	The toy moved. The toy was easy to push; I did not have to use a lot of force.
chair		
book		
pan		
wagon		
paper clip		

Forces and Motion

Forces and Motion

How Much Force?

Write a sentence about each picture.

_____

_____

_____

_____

Do you need to use more force to push a car or a bike? Explain your answer.

_____

_____

Magnets

Look at the picture. Read the word.
Write the word in the sentence.

attract

A magnet will _____, or pull, some kinds of metals.

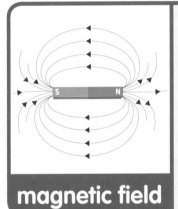
magnetic field

The area around a magnet that attracts objects is called its

_____.

iron

A magnet is attracted to metals that are _____.

Physical Science

Forces at Play

Concept:

Magnets can move things without touching them.

Magnets

A magnet is an object that **attracts** some metals, such as **iron**. The magnet pulls the metal toward it. Steel is a metal with iron, so a magnet will attract something made of steel.

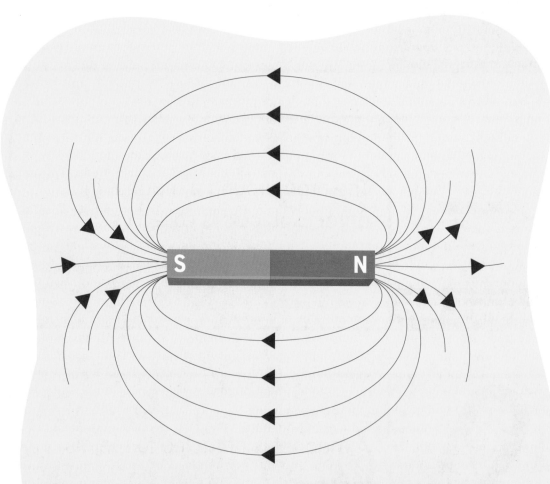

The area around a magnet that attracts magnetic objects is called its **magnetic field**.

A magnet can pull on a metal object without even touching it. It can attract metal even through another material, such as paper or water.

You can probably find magnets all over your home. They hold up papers. They keep doors closed. They are inside computers. Magnets are powerful and useful!

Physical Science

Word Play

Read the clue. Write the word.

1. A kind of metal that is attracted to a magnet

___ ___ ___ ___
 4   1   8

2. To pull in toward itself

___ ___ ___ ___ ___ ___ ___
    7

3. The area around a magnet that pulls in objects

___ ___ ___ ___ ___ ___ ___ ___ ___ ___ ___ ___
  6 5   3   2

Use the numbered letters to solve the puzzle.

Science Puzzle

People put magnets on this item made of steel.

___ ___ ___ ___ ___ ___ ___ ___ ___ ___ ___ ___
 1   2   3   1   4   5   2   1   6   7   8   1

Forces at Play

Magnetic Sentences

Mark the sentence that goes with the picture.

☐ Magnets are different sizes.

☐ Magnets can attract metal through paper.

☐ Magnets attract metals that contain iron.

☐ Magnets are inside computers.

Physical Science

The Force Moves Through

What You Need

- magnet
- paper clip
- piece of cloth
- plastic bag
- wooden ruler
- drinking glass
- foil
- paper

What You Do

1. Put the paper clip on a table. Hold the magnet above it. Bring the magnet closer to the paper clip until you can pick up the paper clip with the magnet.

2. Now put each of the other objects between the magnet and the paper clip. Can you still pick up the paper clip?

3. Record your observations on the record sheet on the next page.

Physical Science

Skill Sharpeners—Science • EMC 5322 • © Evan-Moor Corp.

Object	Does the magnet stick through the object?

Forces at Play

Skill:

Write or draw to demonstrate understanding of science concepts

What Will Stick?

What things will a magnet attract?
Answer with words or drawings.

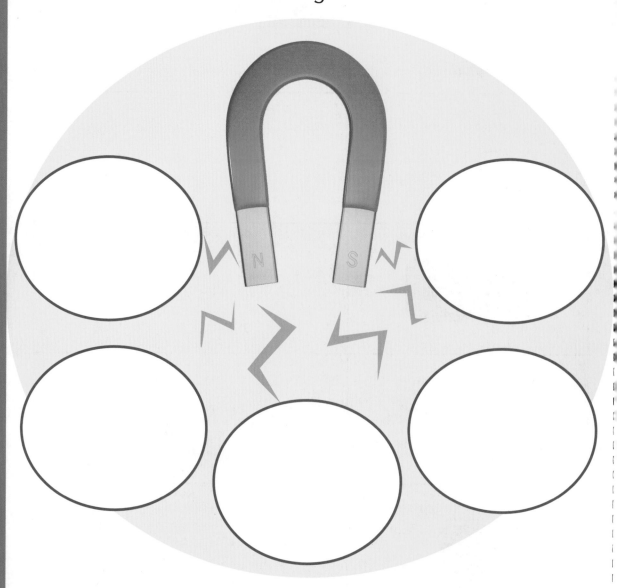

Finish the sentence.

A magnet will attract _____.

Forces at Play

Grow and Change

Look at the picture. Read the word.
Write the word in the sentence.

grow

A child will _____ into an adult.

physical

Changes that happen to your body are called _____ changes.

toddler

A _____ is older than a baby but younger than a child.

My Body

Concept:

People grow and change.

Grow and Change

You **grow** and change in many ways. Some changes are **physical**. Physical changes happen to your body. You get bigger, stronger, and taller.

Another physical change happens to your teeth. You lose your baby teeth to make way for your adult teeth.

You change in other ways, too. You learn to do things you couldn't do before.

When you were a baby, you learned to crawl.

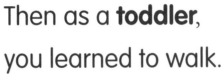

Then as a **toddler**, you learned to walk.

Then you learned to ride a bike. You are always learning. What else will you learn to do as you grow?

Life Science

My Body

Then and Now

Write a word to go with the picture. Then draw a line to match then and now.

| crawl | eat | talk | jump | drink | cry |

Then

Now

_____

_____

_____

_____

_____

_____

Moving Along

Write **1, 2, 3, 4** to order the pictures.

Finish each sentence.

1. First, a baby _____.

2. Then, a toddler learns to _____.

3. After that, a child can _____ a bike.

4. Finally, an adult can _____ a car.

My Body

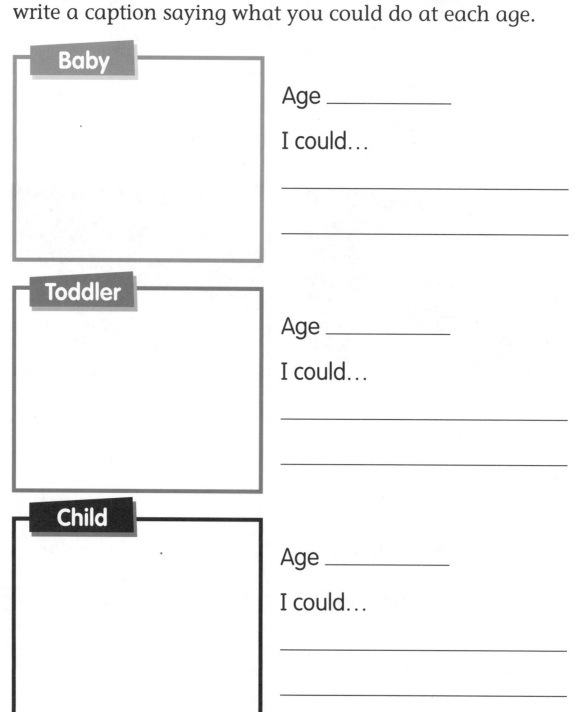

Create a Timeline

Using photos or drawings, make a timeline that shows you as a baby, a toddler, and a child. Include your age, and write a caption saying what you could do at each age.

Baby

Age _____

I could…

_____

_____

Toddler

Age _____

I could…

_____

_____

Child

Age _____

I could…

_____

_____

My Body

Hand in Hand

Make a colorful handprint picture with an adult!

What You Need

- paint
- construction paper
- paper plates

What You Do

1. Choose which paint colors you will use. Pour a small amount of each paint color on a paper plate.

2. Place a large piece of construction paper on a table.

3. Dip your palm in the paint and press your hand onto the paper. Then dip your fingers into the paint and press them onto the paper.

4. Have an adult do the same thing with his or her hand.

5. Look at both handprints. Talk about how they are different in size.

Write how your handprint will change over time.

_____

_____

My Body

Skill:

Record information in charts or graphs

Growth and Change Chart

Have you gotten taller? Do you weigh more? Have you learned to do something you couldn't do last year?

Complete the chart to answer these questions. Ask a parent or guardian for help if you can't remember.

	Last Year	Now
Height		
Weight		
Play		
Learn		

My Body

Bones and Joints

Look at the picture. Read the word.
Write the word in the sentence.

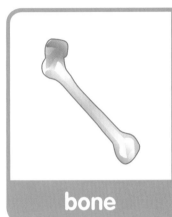

bone

Each _____ in your body is strong.

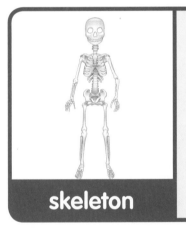

skeleton

All the bones together are called a _____.

joint

Each _____ in your body helps you to bend.

Life Science

Body Parts

Concept:

Bones and joints help support and move your body.

Body Parts

Bones and Joints

Your body has many **bones**. All the bones together form a **skeleton**. Your skeleton helps you stand up and move. When you are all grown up, you will have 206 bones in your skeleton.

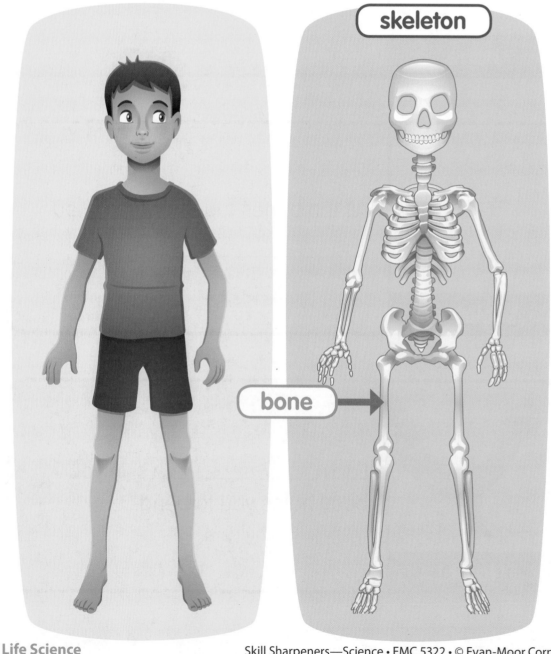

skeleton

bone

Bend your fingers. Bones can't bend, so how are you able to bend your fingers? Your fingers bend because of **joints**. Your joints help you bend, turn, and twist. Joints are where the bones in your body come together.

joints

Word Play

Read the clue. Write the word.

1. You will have 206 of these when you grow up.

   ___ ___ ___ ___
        3

2. All the bones in your body make up your

   ___ ___ ___ ___ ___ ___ ___ ___.
                      2

3. These help you twist.

   ___ ___ ___ ___ ___ ___
                      1

Write the numbered letters to solve the puzzle.

Science Puzzle

Bones and joints help you

___ ___ a ___ d up and move.
 1   2   3

Body Parts

Skill:
Interpret information from graphic images

Your Bones

Different bones have different names.

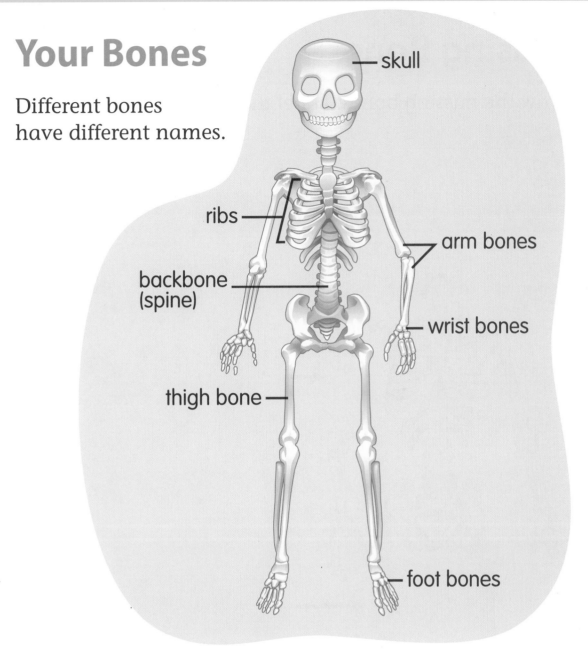

- skull
- ribs
- arm bones
- backbone (spine)
- wrist bones
- thigh bone
- foot bones

Look at the skeleton. Name these bones.

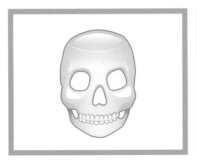

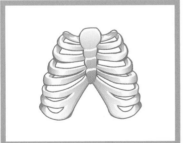

_____ _____ _____

Life Science

Body Parts

Missing Bones

Draw the missing bones. Label them.

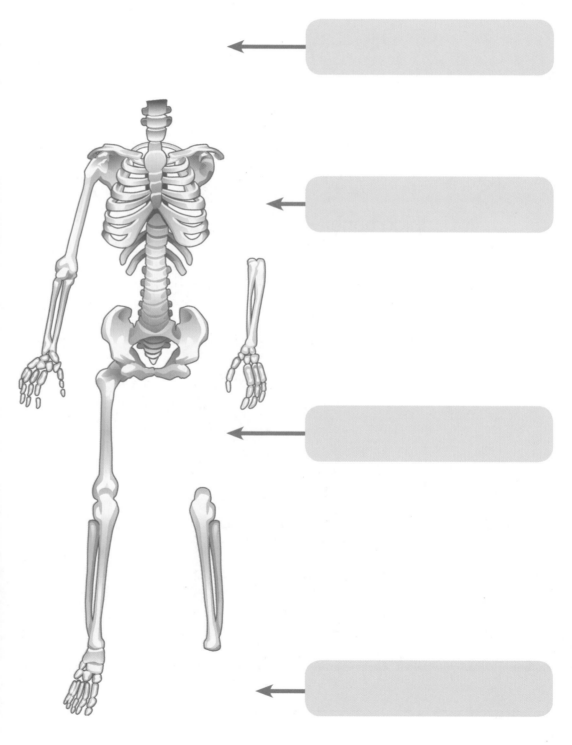

Sweet and Salty Skeleton

Use pretzels, frosting, and marshmallows to make a hand!

Skill:

Make projects to demonstrate understanding of science concepts

What You Need

- 1 cup (125 g) powdered sugar
- 4 tablespoons (56 g) softened butter
- pretzel sticks
- ½ tablespoon (7 mL) water
- mini marshmallows, cut in half
- wax paper

What You Do

1. Lay a piece of wax paper over this picture of a hand.

2. Mix the sugar, butter, and water to make frosting.

3. Dip the pretzel sticks in the frosting and place them on the piece of wax paper in the shape of the hand.

4. Place mini marshmallows between the frosted pretzels to make joints.

5. Enjoy this tasty treat!

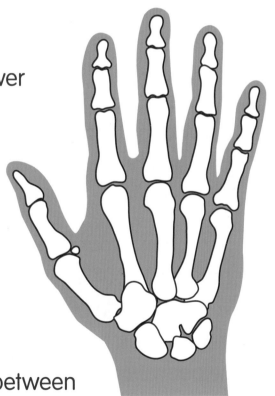

Body Parts

Skill:
Conduct science experiments and record results

Red Dot Joints

1. Sit down on a chair. Straighten one leg so that your foot comes off the floor. Now look at the skeleton. Draw a red dot on the joint that just helped you straighten your leg.

2. Now stand up. Put your arm straight out without bending at the elbow. Move your arm in a circle at the shoulder. Draw a red dot on the joint that helped you circle your arm.

3. Next, bend your knee and raise your leg. Circle your leg at the hip. Draw a red dot on the joint that helped you circle your leg at the hip.

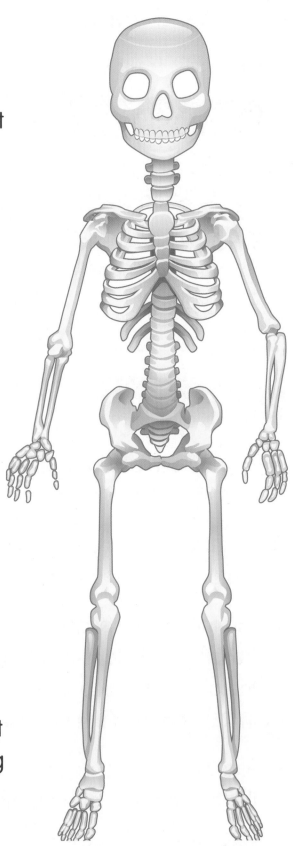

Body Parts

Animals Grow and Change

Look at the picture. Read the word.
Write the word in the sentence.

mammals

_____ are animals that grow inside their mothers and drink their milk.

chick

A baby bird is called a

_____.

hatch

A chick will _____ from an egg.

life cycle

The parts of an animal's life from birth to death are called its

_____.

Animal Life Cycles

Concept:

Animals grow and change.

Animal Life Cycles

Animals Grow and Change

Look at this mother cat and her kittens.

Cats are **mammals**. This means that mother cats grow their kittens inside their bodies. When the kittens are born, they are weak. The kittens drink milk from their mother's body. This is how it is with most mammals, including humans.

Mother cat grows kittens inside her.

Kittens grow into cats.

Kittens are born.

Kittens drink mother's milk.

Look at this mother hen and her chick.

Life begins differently for **chicks**. This is because chickens are not mammals. A hen lays her eggs in a nest. The chicks break the eggs and **hatch**. They will grow into adult chickens, and the **life cycle** will continue.

Mother hen lays eggs.

Chicks grow inside the eggs.

Chicks hatch.

Chicks grow into adult chickens.

Word Play

Read the clue. Write the word.

1. Baby bird

   ___ ___ ___ ___
    1   4

2. Animals that grow inside their mothers

   ___ ___ ___ ___ ___ ___ ___
    2

3. A baby mammal drinks this from its mother.

   ___ ___ ___ ___

4. A place where hens lay their eggs

   ___ ___ ___
    5   6   3

Write the numbered letters to solve the puzzle.

Science Puzzle

The egg breaks and the chick

___ ___ ___ ___ ___ ___ ___ .
 1   2   3   4   1   5   6

Animal Life Cycles

Waiting to Hatch

Chicks stay inside eggs for different amounts of time. The amount of time each chick stays in the egg depends on the size of the mother bird.

goose
30 days

chicken
21 days

hummingbird
16 days

Animal Life Cycles

1. Which of the three chicks takes the longest to hatch? _____

2. Which takes longer to hatch, a chicken or a hummingbird? _____

3. Explain why a goose takes 14 more days to hatch than a hummingbird.

_____

_____

Animal Life Cycles

Clay Animals

Use clay to make models of a mother animal and its baby.

What You Need

- modeling clay
- paintbrush
- different colors of paint

What You Do

1. Choose your favorite animal to research. Look in books or on the Internet to find out about the animal's life cycle—how it grows from a baby to an adult.

2. Use the modeling clay to make a model of your favorite mother and baby animal.

3. Use your fingers and a tool such as a toothpick or chopstick to add details to the animals.

4. Let the clay dry, and then paint the animals.

5. Complete the form on the next page to tell about your favorite animal.

Write about the clay animal that you made.

The animal I made is a _____.

The baby is called a _____.

It lives in _____.

It eats _____.

It sleeps _____.

Write a sentence about this animal's life cycle.

_____

_____

_____

Circle the correct answers to show if the animal is a mammal.

1. The baby grows   **in its mother   in an egg**.

2. The baby   **does   does not**   drink its mother's milk.

3. Is the animal a mammal?   **yes   no**

Animal Life Cycles

Skill:

Complete charts or graphs to demonstrate understanding of science concepts

Animal Life Cycles

Cat and Bird

Write to describe each stage of the life cycle.

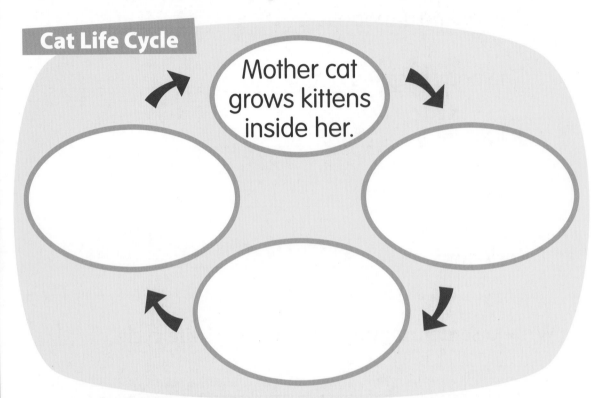

Cat Life Cycle

Mother cat grows kittens inside her.

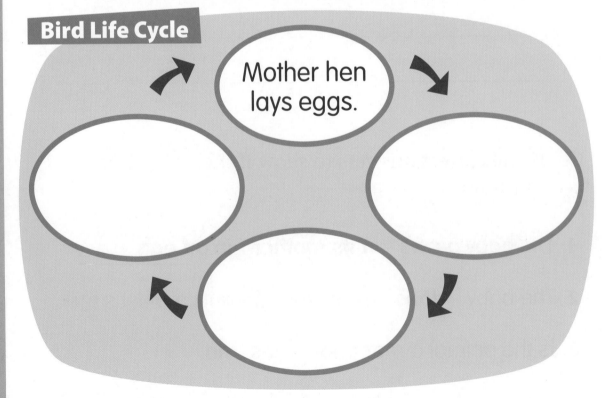

Bird Life Cycle

Mother hen lays eggs.

Skill Sharpeners—Science • EMC 5322 • © Evan-Moor Corp.

Plants Grow and Change

Look at the picture. Read the word.
Write the word in the sentence.

roots

The _____ grow into the ground.

stem

The _____ is the part that connects the roots and the leaves.

shoot

A _____ grows up out of the soil.

pod

A _____ holds many seeds.

Plants

Concept:

Plants grow
and change.

From Seed to Plant

A seed is the start of a new plant.

How does a seed grow into a plant?

A bean seed is planted
in the ground. A tiny new
plant is inside the seed.

shoot

stem

roots

The seedcase splits open.
A tiny **root** starts to grow
down into the ground. A
shoot begins to sprout up
out of the soil.

The plant's **stem**
grows longer, and
leaves grow on the
stem. Leaves make
food for the plant.

Plants

pod

Flowers bloom among the leaves. The flowers make seed pods.

Day by day, the bean plant grows. First it is a seedling, or baby plant. As it grows, flowers bloom among the leaves. Soon these flowers will make seeds.

After most of the flowers are gone, seed **pods** appear. When the pods open, the seeds fall out into the ground.

Then the plant cycle starts all over again. The new seeds grow into plants.

Word Play

Read the clue. Write the word.

1. A plant starts with a ___ ___ ___ ___.
   ₃

2. When the stem grows longer, these grow on the plant.

   ___ ___ ___ ___ ___
   ₄

3. Where seeds are planted

   ___ ___ ___ ___
   2   1

4. The part of the plant that grows down into the ground

   ___ ___ ___ ___

Write the numbered letters to solve the puzzle.

Science Puzzle

A seed has a tiny plant

___ n ___ ___ ___ ___ of it.
1   2   1   3   4

Plants

Pumpkin Life Cycle

Skill:

Interpret information from graphic images

Look at each picture below. Then write the letter of the sentence that matches that picture.

a. It has many leaves, and flowers grow on the plant.

b. A pumpkin seed is planted.

c. The big orange pumpkin is filled with seeds.

d. A root grows down. A shoot grows up.

Plants

Life Cycle of a Pea

You can watch pea seeds grow into plants with flowers.
When the flowers make pea pods, open them and plant
the seeds. The cycle will be complete!

What You Need

- pea seeds
- soil
- clear cup

What You Do

1. Soak two or three pea seeds in water overnight.

2. Plant the pea seeds in the clear cup filled with soil. Put the seeds up against the side of the cup.

3. Water the seeds and place the cup in a warm and sunny place.

4. Water the soil whenever it becomes dry.

5. As the plant grows, measure it. Record what you see in the chart on the next page.

Plants

Fill in the chart.

Week	How tall?	How many flowers?	How many seed pods?
Week 1			
Week 2			
Week 3			
Week 4			
Week 5			
Week 6			
Week 7			
Week 8			

Plants

Skill:

Write sentences to demonstrate understanding of science concepts

Pea Plant Life Cycle

Label the picture of the plant life cycle.

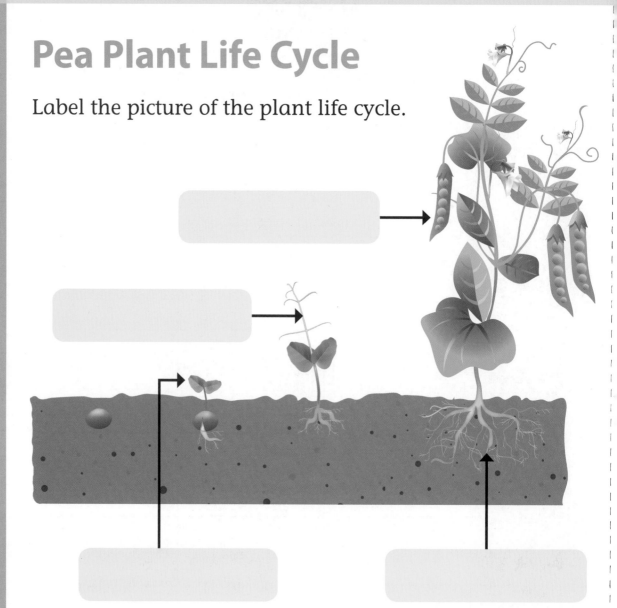

Write to tell about it.

_____

_____

_____

_____

Ocean and Desert

Look at the picture. Read the word.
Write the word in the sentence.

ocean

The _____ is a large body of salt water where many plants and animals live.

desert

The _____ gets very little rainfall.

cactus

A _____ has a thick stem that stores water when it rains.

habitat

A _____ is a place where plants and animals live.

Life Science

Habitats

Concept:
Habitats have all kinds of life.

Ocean and Desert Habitats

A **habitat** is a place where plants and animals live. An **ocean** is a habitat. Plants grow in ocean water that gets sunlight.

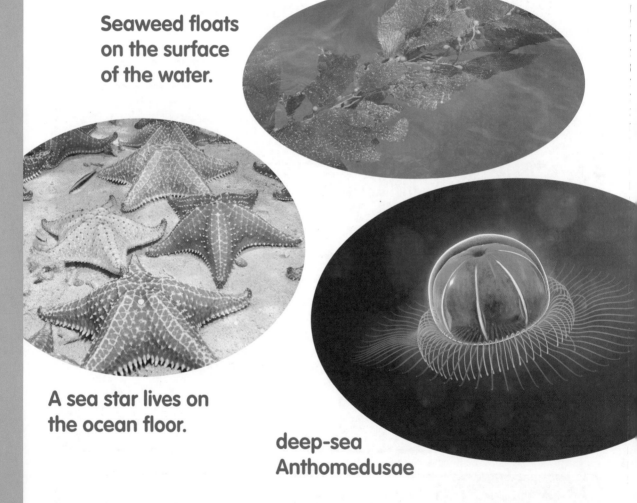

Seaweed floats on the surface of the water.

A sea star lives on the ocean floor.

deep-sea Anthomedusae

Many interesting animals live in the ocean. They live in all parts of the water, from the shallow coast to the ocean floor. Some animals even live in water so deep that there is no light.

Habitats

The **desert** is the driest habitat. But plants and animals have found ways to live in this hot and dry habitat.

Many desert plants can go a long time without water. The **cactus** has a thick stem that stores water when it rains.

cactus

Many desert animals get water from the plants or seeds they eat. They have also found ways to deal with the heat. Some animals rest in the shade. Others live underground and go out only at night when it is cooler.

A kangaroo rat goes out only at night.

Habitats

Word Play

Read the clue. Write the word.

1. Some desert animals come out only

   at __ __ __ __ __.

2. The wettest habitat is the

   __ __ __ __ __.
            1

3. The driest habitat is the

   __ __ __ __ __.
   2

4. The __ __ __ __ __ __ is a desert
              4

   __ __ __ __ __ that stores water in its stem.
   3

Write the numbered letters to solve the puzzle.

Science Puzzle

Plants and animals __ __ __ __ __,
                1   2   1   3   4

or change, to fit in to their habitats.

Habitats

Compare the Ocean and Desert

Skill:

Interpret information from charts or graphs

Read the diagram.

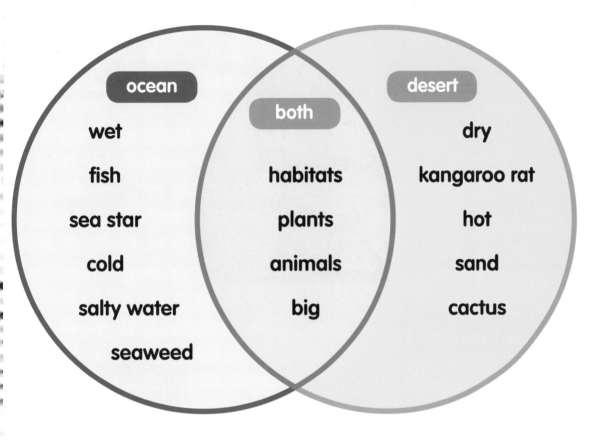

ocean
wet
fish
sea star
cold
salty water
seaweed

both
habitats
plants
animals
big

desert
dry
kangaroo rat
hot
sand
cactus

How are the ocean and desert the same?

_____

_____

How are the ocean and desert different?

_____

_____

Habitats

Paper Ocean

Make a 3-D ocean out of paper.

What You Need

- rectangle of blue paper
- craft decorations (ribbon, yarn, stickers, glitter, paper, etc.)
- scissors
- glue

What You Do

1. Fold the rectangle in half, bringing the short ends of the blue paper together. Starting at the folded end, cut wavy lines across to the other side, stopping just before you get to the edge.

2. Open the paper and separate the waves, as shown.

3. Using the craft decorations, create plants and animals and put them in the ocean.

Habitats

Make a Cactus

A saguaro cactus has sweet red fruit. All kinds of desert animals eat this fruit. You can make a mini saguaro out of clay.

What You Need

- picture of saguaro cactus
- saucer filled with rice, peas, or lentils
- green modeling clay
- red beads
- toothpicks
- fork

What You Do

1. Shape the clay into a cactus. Use the fork to make grooves.

2. Add red beads to represent ripe fruit ready for eating. Use the toothpicks to make prickly needles. When you are finished, display your cactus in the saucer with rice or dried lentils.

Habitats

Skill:

Complete charts or graphs to demonstrate understanding of science concepts

Ocean and Desert Life

Write the names of plants and animals that you can find in the ocean and the desert.

| fish | seaweed | cactus |
| kangaroo rat | lizard | sea star |

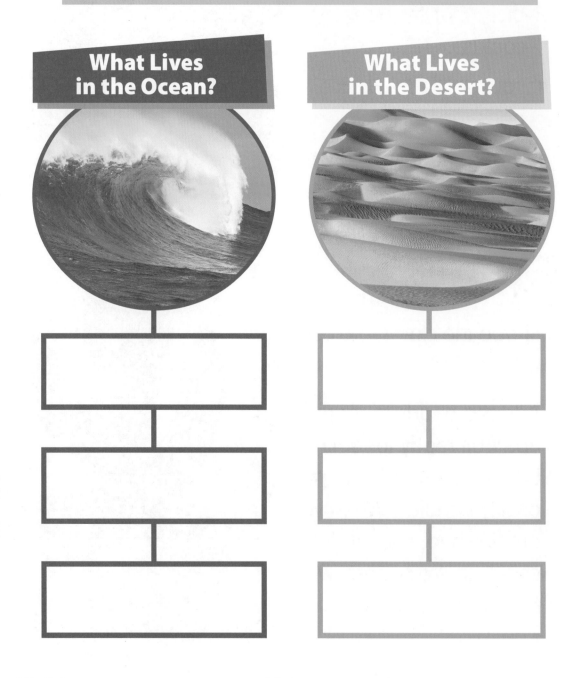

What Lives in the Ocean?

What Lives in the Desert?

Habitats

Moon and Stars

Look at the picture. Read the word.
Write the word in the sentence.

moon

The _____ reflects light from the sun.

crescent

A _____ shows only part of the moon.

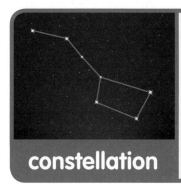

star

A _____ is a ball of hot gases.

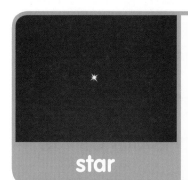

constellation

A _____ is a pattern of stars.

Space

Concept:

We can see the objects in the sky.

We See the Moon

new moon   crescent moon   quarter moon   full moon

Space

What do we see in the sky at night? We see the moon. The **moon** does not make its own light. It reflects the light from the sun.

The moon is always round, but we do not see all of it every night. As the moon travels around Earth, it looks different to us. It starts out as the new moon. As the moon moves, its shape looks like a **crescent**. By the time the moon travels all the way around Earth, it looks like a round, full moon. The changes in the shape of the moon that we see are called **phases**.

We See Stars

North Star

Little Dipper

Big Dipper

A star is a ball of hot gases. **Stars** make light and heat. Stars are so far away from Earth that we cannot feel their heat. The stars just look like tiny dots of light.

You can see about 2,000 stars with your eyes. Long ago, people gave names to groups of stars. These groups of stars are called **constellations**.

Word Play

Read the clue. Write the word.

1. Big, round moon

___ ___ ___ ___ ___ ___ ___ ___
       6

2. Look like tiny dots of light

___ ___ ___ ___ ___
     7   3

3. The planet you are on

___ ___ ___ ___ ___
5   4

4. The moon when it is shaped like a banana

___ ___ ___ ___ ___ ___ ___ ___ ___ ___ ___
1   2

Write the numbered letters to solve the puzzle.

Science Puzzle

The Big Dipper is a

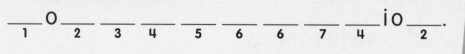

___ o ___ ___ ___ ___ ___ ___ i o ___.
1 2 3 4 5 6 6 7 4   2

Phases

Write the name of each phase of the moon.

Skill:

Label graphic images to demonstrate understanding of science concepts

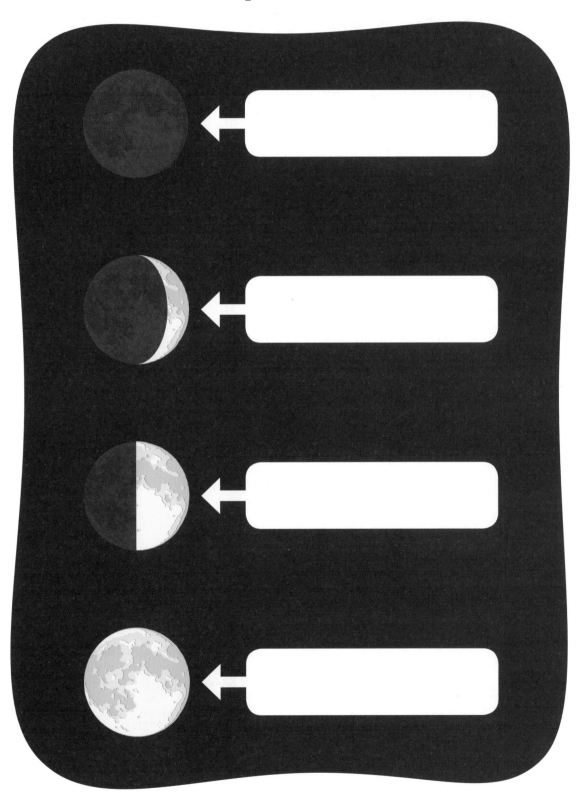

Cookie Moon

Show the phases of the moon using sandwich cookies.

What You Need

- 8 sandwich cookies
- spoon
- paper plate

What You Do

1. Twist open the cookies. Use only the sides that have filling. Set aside the other sides, except for one, which will be used as the new moon.

2. Use the spoon to scrape off the filling so that each cookie looks like a phase of the moon.

3. Arrange the cookies on a paper plate. Label each cookie with the name of a phase: **new moon**, **crescent moon**, **quarter moon**, and **full moon**.

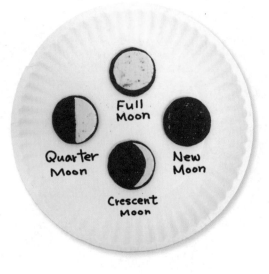

Space

Stars in a Jar

See the Big Dipper constellation on your wall!

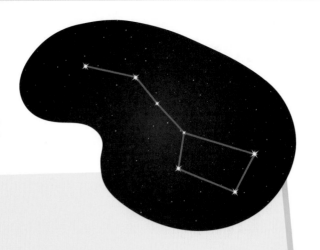

What You Need

- picture of Big Dipper
- black paper
- clear jar
- glow stick
- sharpened pencil
- thumbtack
- chalk or white crayon

What You Do

1. Cut the black paper so that it will fit like a cylinder inside the jar.

2. Using chalk or a white crayon, draw the Big Dipper on the black paper.

3. Poke holes in each star of the constellation. Use a pencil for big stars and a thumbtack for tiny stars.

4. Bend the black paper into a cylinder shape. Tape it closed. Place it inside the jar.

5. Put a glow stick inside the cylinder. Turn off the lights, and the constellation will appear on your wall!

Moon and Stars

Draw a line to match.

crescent moon	ball of hot gases
full moon	slice of moon
star	pattern of stars
constellation	changes in the moon
phases	big, round moon

Space

Skill Sharpeners—Science • EMC 5322 • © Evan-Moor Corp.

Look at the picture. Read the word.
Write the word in the sentence.

sun

The _____ is a ball
of hot gases.

Earth

_____ travels
around the sun.

plants

The sun helps _____
grow.

The Sun

We Need the Sun

The **sun** is an object in the sky. The sun is a ball of hot gases. It is the star that is closest to Earth. It is the star we see in the daytime.

The sun is much bigger than **Earth**. The sun looks small because it is so far away. Earth travels around the sun. It takes one year for Earth to travel all the way around the sun.

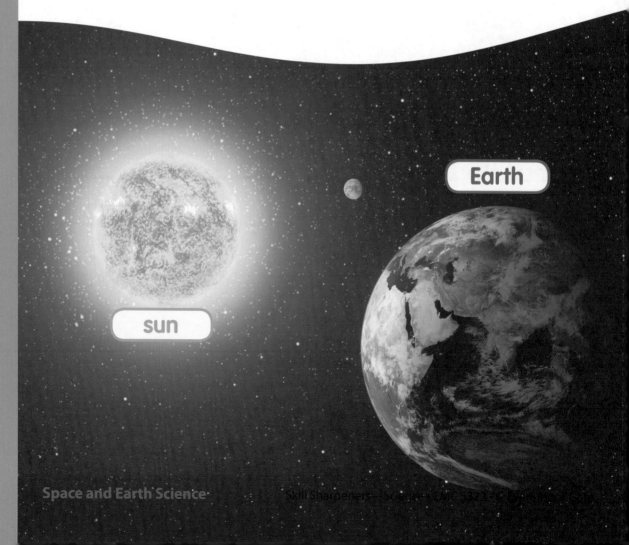

Earth

sun

The Sun

People need the sun. It gives us heat to stay warm. It gives us light to see.

Plants need the sun, too. The sun helps plants make their food. Plants make oxygen for people and animals to breathe.

Without the sun, people, plants, and animals could not live on Earth.

The Sun

Space and Earth Science

Word Play

Read the clue. Write the word.

1. The star closest to Earth

   ___ ___ ___
            1

2. The sun gives off this so you can see.

   ___ ___ ___ ___ ___
        2   3

3. The time it takes for Earth to travel all the way around the sun

   ___ ___ ___ ___

4. The sun gives us this to stay warm.

   ___ ___ ___ ___
    4   5

Write the numbered letters to solve the puzzle.

Science Puzzle

We cannot see the sun at

___ ___ ___ ___ ___.
 1   2   3   4   5

The Sun

The Sun

Skill:

Write sentences to demonstrate understanding of science concepts

Look at this picture. Write about how the sun helps people, plants, and animals on Earth.

_____

_____

_____

_____

_____

Sun Picture

See how the light from the sun can cause changes.

What You Need

- tape
- foam stickers or shapes
- dark construction paper

What You Do

1. Arrange the shapes on the construction paper.

2. Tape the construction paper to a sunny window, facing out.

3. After a week, take down the construction paper and remove the shapes. Look at the construction paper and answer the question.

What did the sun do to the construction paper?

_____

_____

Skill Sharpeners—Science • EMC 5322 • © Evan-Moor Corp.

Blended Suncatcher

Catch the sun with a disk that hangs in a window.

Skill:

Make art projects to represent science concepts

What You Need

- glitter beads in see-through colors
- disposable pie pan
- parchment paper

What You Do

1. Cut a circle of parchment paper to fit the bottom of the pie pan. Line the pan with the paper.

2. Ask an adult to preheat the oven to 375°F (190°C).

3. Arrange the beads on the parchment paper so that they look like a sun.

4. Place the pan in the oven for about 20 minutes or until the beads are melted.

5. Take the pan of melted beads out of the oven (an adult's job). Let them cool.

6. Pop the disk out of the pan. Drill a hole at the top (an adult's job).

7. String yarn through the hole and hang the sun in a window. Watch your bead sun catch the real sun!

The Sun

Skill:

Write sentences to demonstrate understanding of science concepts

Sun Facts

Write to tell what you learned about the sun.

What is the sun?

_____

_____

Why does the sun look small?

_____

_____

How does the sun help people, plants, and animals?

_____

_____

The Sun

Clouds

Look at the picture. Read the word.
Write the word in the sentence.

precipitation

_____ can be rain, snow, or ice.

cumulus

A _____ cloud is fluffy.

stratus

A _____ cloud makes the sky gray.

cirrus

A _____ cloud is thin like a feather.

Weather

We See Clouds

Concept:

Different cloud types give us different weather.

When we look up at the sky, we see clouds. Some clouds look like cotton balls. Some clouds look like a gray blanket. Other clouds look like white feathers.

How do clouds form? Tiny droplets of water or pieces of ice hang in the air. The water or ice bunches together and forms a cloud.

precipitation

When the water or ice gets too heavy, it falls to the ground. The moisture that falls to Earth is called **precipitation**. Precipitation can be rain, snow, or ice.

Weather

Here are three kinds of clouds you might see:

cumulus

Cumulus clouds are fluffy and piled up high. You can see these clouds on warm, sunny days.

stratus

Stratus clouds hang low and flat, like a gray blanket. Sometimes stratus clouds send down a light drizzle or a sprinkle of rain.

cirrus

Cirrus clouds are made of ice crystals. They are thin, curly wisps high in the sky.

Weather

Skill:

Apply content
vocabulary in
context

Word Play

Read the clue. Write the word.

1. Stratus clouds sometimes rest on the

   ground as ___ ___ ___.
    1

2. Wispy cloud

   ___ ___ ___ ___ ___ ___
    2

3. A form of precipitation

   ___ ___ ___ ___
    3

4. Cirrus clouds are made of

   ice ___ ___ ___ ___ ___ ___ ___ ___.
    4

Write the numbered letters to solve the puzzle.

Science Puzzle

Stratus clouds make the sky look

___ ___ ___ ___.
1 2 3 4

Weather

Cloud Names

Write the name of each cloud.

Skill:
Label graphic images to demonstrate understanding of science concepts

cirrus   stratus   cumulus

Weather

Skill:
Conduct experiments and answer questions

Cloud in a Glass

Make a cumulus cloud in a glass and then make it rain.

What You Need

- shaving cream
- clear glass
- water
- blue food coloring

What You Do

1. Fill the glass halfway with water.

2. Pile a mound of shaving cream on top of the water in the glass. Make it look like a fluffy cumulus cloud.

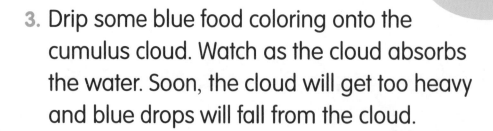

3. Drip some blue food coloring onto the cumulus cloud. Watch as the cloud absorbs the water. Soon, the cloud will get too heavy and blue drops will fall from the cloud.

How is this similar to how rain really happens?

_____

_____

Weather

Cloud Dough

Skill:

Make art projects to represent science concepts

Form different types of clouds using this special dough.

What You Need

- 2 cups (250 g) white flour
- ¼ cup (60 mL) oil, such as baby oil or vegetable oil
- black paint (for stratus clouds)
- 3 sheets blue construction paper

What You Do

1. Mix the flour and oil to make the basic cloud dough. You can use this dough to make cumulus and cirrus clouds.

2. Take out about one-third of the dough. Add a little black paint to it and mix. You can use this gray dough to make stratus clouds.

3. Label each construction paper sheet: cirrus, stratus, cumulus.

4. Form one type of cloud on each paper. Tell someone about the different clouds.

Cirrus

stratus

Cumulus

weather

Word Cloud

Next to each picture, write the name of the cloud you learned about. Then write two words to describe each cloud.

name

_____

_____

name

_____

_____

name

_____

_____

Land Changes

Look at the picture. Read the word.
Write the word in the sentence.

erosion

_____ carries
away rock and soil.

weathering

_____ breaks
down or wears away rock.

surface

People also shape the
_____ of
the land.

Earth's Systems

Geology

Concept:
Different forces shape the land.

How Does the Land Change?

Earth's **surface** changes over time. It takes many years and different forces to cause these changes.

Erosion is a force that shapes the land. Erosion happens when rock and soil are carried away by water and wind. For example, a stream can carry away rock and soil and carve a path in the land. Over time, erosion might turn that path into a canyon. That's how the Grand Canyon was formed!

Weathering is also a force that shapes the land. Weathering happens when water or wind break down or wear away rock. Have you ever found a smooth rock on the beach? That is an example of weathering.

Skill Sharpeners—Science • EMC 5322 • © Evan-Moor Corp.

Weathering and erosion are two natural forces that change the land. But people can change the land, too. Walking or riding along the same path wears the land down. Building roads changes the land, and so does planting crops and trees.

In nature, things are always changing. Water, wind, and people cause some of these changes to happen.

Skill:

Apply science vocabulary in context

Word Play

Read the clue. Write the word.

1. This part of Earth changes over time.

   __ __ __ __ __ __
            1   5

2. This carries rock and soil away.

   __ __ __ __ __ __ __
       2

3. The wearing away of rock is called

   __ __ __ __ __ __ __ __ __.
                 3

4. Nature doesn't stay the same; it

   __ __ __ __ __ __.
   4   6

Write the numbered letters to solve the puzzle.

Science Puzzle

The land is changed by different

__ __ __ __ __ __.
1 2 3 4 5 6

Geology

Skill Sharpeners—Science • EMC 5322 • © Evan-Moor Corp.

What Happened?

This is a picture of a road that is being built. People had to change the land to make room for the road. What are some things you think people did to change the land? Choose all that apply.

☐ Cut down trees

☐ Planted more trees

☐ Dug up big rocks

☐ Dug a big hole

☐ Made the land flat

Geology

's Systems

Skill:
Conduct
experiments
and answer
questions

Weathering Rocks

Rocks in a stream become weathered when they are tumbled by the water. Here is how you can weather rocks yourself.

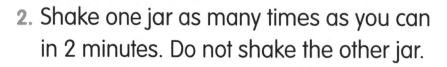

What You Need

- handful of gravel
- 2 small jars with tight lids
- 2 coffee filters
- strainer
- bowl
- water

What You Do

1. Place half the gravel in each jar, and fill the jars with water.

2. Shake one jar as many times as you can in 2 minutes. Do not shake the other jar.

3. Place a coffee filter inside the strainer. Hold it over the bowl. Pour everything from the jar you shook into the filter. Let the water drain.

4. Take the rocks out of the filter, but leave the sand. Then lay the sandy filter flat to dry.

5. Repeat Steps 3 and 4 with the unshaken jar.

Why did one filter have more sand?

_____

_____

Soil Erosion

Skill:
Conduct experiments and record results

Explore how wind and water move soil.

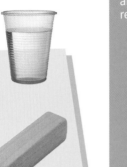

What You Need

- disposable plate
- dry soil or sand
- piece of wood
- cup of water

What You Do

1. Work outside (in the yard or at the beach) for easy cleanup.

2. Sprinkle some soil (or sand) on the plate.

3. Blow on the soil. What happened to it?

_____

4. Now use the wood to prop up the plate.

5. Pour water on the soil. What happened to the soil?

_____

_____

6. How might you keep the soil from being blown or washed away?

_____

_____

Geology

Skill:

Label graphic images to demonstrate understanding of science concepts

Erosion, Weathering, or People?

What made the change? Write *erosion*, *weathering*, or *people*.

Geology

Water on Earth

Look at the picture. Read the word.
Write the word in the sentence.

salt water

Most of Earth's water is
_____.

glacier

A _____ is made of frozen fresh water.

fresh water

_____ is the water we can drink.

iceberg

An _____ is ice that floats in the ocean.

Water and Ice

Water and Ice

Earth's Water

About 70 percent of Earth's surface is covered with water. This water is in both liquid and solid form.

Almost all of the liquid water on Earth is **salt water**. This is water in the ocean. We cannot use salt water. We need fresh water for drinking, washing, and cooking. But only a tiny amount of Earth's water is **fresh water**. Some can be found in rivers and lakes. Other fresh water is underground.

fresh water

glacier

A huge amount of fresh water is locked up inside glaciers. A **glacier** is a thick sheet of ice that forms on land. Glaciers actually move, though very slowly.

Sometimes a huge chunk of ice will break away from a glacier and float into the sea. This floating ice is called an **iceberg**. As it floats, only the tip of the iceberg shows. The rest is underwater.

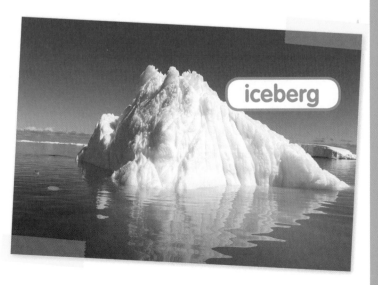

iceberg

water and ice

Word Play

Read the clue. Write the word.

1. Water in the ocean

   $\underline{\quad}$ $\underline{\quad}$ $\underline{\quad}$ $\underline{\quad}$ $\underline{\quad}$ $\underline{\quad}$ $\underline{\quad}$ $\underline{\quad}$ $\underline{\quad}$
     4   3

2. A sheet of ice on land

   $\underline{\quad}$ $\underline{\quad}$ $\underline{\quad}$ $\underline{\quad}$ $\underline{\quad}$ $\underline{\quad}$
                   1

3. Ice floating in the ocean

   $\underline{\quad}$ $\underline{\quad}$ $\underline{\quad}$ $\underline{\quad}$ $\underline{\quad}$ $\underline{\quad}$ $\underline{\quad}$
      2

4. Water you can drink

   $\underline{\quad}$ $\underline{\quad}$ $\underline{\quad}$ $\underline{\quad}$ $\underline{\quad}$ $\underline{\quad}$ $\underline{\quad}$ $\underline{\quad}$ $\underline{\quad}$
                5   6

Write the numbered letters to solve the puzzle.

Science Puzzle

A very large glacier is called an

$\underline{\quad}$ $\underline{\quad}$ $\underline{\quad}$ $\underline{\quad}$ $\underline{\quad}$ $\underline{\quad}$ $\underline{\quad}$ $\underline{\quad}$.
 1   2   3   4   5   3   3   6

Water and Ice

Water and Ice

Write the name of each type of Earth's water.

| glacier | iceberg | fresh water | salt water |

Skill:
Label graphic images to demonstrate understanding of science concepts

Water and Ice

Skill:

Conduct experiments

Moving Glacier

Glaciers move very slowly across the land. You can make your own glacier to help you see how these large sheets of ice move.

What You Need

- resealable plastic bag
- 3 tablespoons (44 mL) warm water
- 1 tablespoon (14 mL) white glue
- 2 tablespoons (28 mL) borax
- drop of blue food coloring
- mixing bowl

What You Do

1. Mix the water and glue in the plastic bag.

2. Add the borax and close the bag. Knead the mixture until it comes together.

3. Open the bag and add a drop of blue food coloring. Mix until the mixture is blue.

4. Set the bowl upside down. This is a mountain. Empty the mixture onto the mountaintop. Watch it creep slowly downhill, the way a glacier would move.

Water and ice

Mini Iceberg

Make a mini iceberg and watch it float.

What You Need

- resealable plastic sandwich bag
- water
- jar with lid
- clear bowl

What You Do

1. Fill the sandwich bag halfway with water.

2. Hold the bag so the water is in a corner. Seal the bag shut.

3. Place the bag inside the jar. Let the end of the bag hang over the top of the jar.

4. Screw the lid on the jar, trapping the end of the bag.

5. Place the jar in the freezer overnight.

6. The next day, remove the mini iceberg from the bag.

7. Fill a bowl with water. Place the mini iceberg in the water.

8. How much of the iceberg is above water? How much is below?

water and ice

Skill:

Write sentences to demonstrate understanding of science concepts

Types of Water and Ice

In the boxes below, write the names of the two types of water and ice you learned about, and describe them.

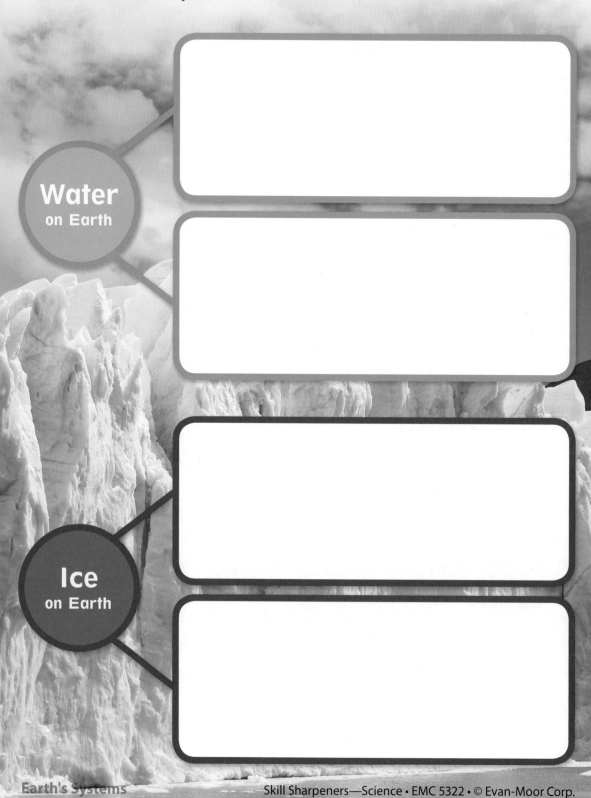

Water on Earth

Ice on Earth

Earth's Systems

Skill Sharpeners—Science • EMC 5322 • © Evan-Moor Corp.

Water and Ice

Scientists

Look at the picture. Read the word.
Write the word in the sentence.

scientist

A _____ studies the world to find out how it works.

botanist

A _____ is a scientist who studies plants.

zoologist

A _____ is a scientist who studies animals.

meteorologist

A _____ is a scientist who studies weather.

Science

Concept:

Scientists make observations, conduct experiments, gather information, and draw conclusions about the world.

Learning about Scientists

People who study the world to find out how it works are called scientists. In order to learn about the world, scientists ask questions and conduct experiments. They take the information from the experiment and think about the results, or what it tells them. Information that a scientist discovers may be used to solve real-life problems like protecting the environment or finding a cure for a disease.

Science

Science and Engineering

Skill Sharpeners—Science • EMC 5322 • © Evan-Moor Corp.

Scientists study many different things and work in many different places.

A scientist who studies plants like trees and flowers is a botanist.

A scientist who studies animals is a zoologist.

A scientist who studies the weather is a meteorologist.

One thing all scientists have in common is that they make important discoveries and they help us better understand the world.

Science

Word Play

Read the clue. Write the word.

1. A scientist who studies animals

    ___ ___ ___ ___ ___ ___ ___ ___
        2

2. What a meteorologist studies

    ___ ___ ___ ___ ___ ___ ___
    1

3. Scientists conduct these.

    ___ ___ ___ ___ ___ ___ ___ ___ ___ ___ ___
                      3

4. Scientists solve these problems.

    ___ ___ ___ ___ - ___ ___ ___ ___
                    4

5. Scientists make these by doing experiments.

    ___ ___ ___ ___ ___ ___ ___ ___ ___ ___ ___
    5

Write the numbered letters to solve the puzzle.

Science Puzzle

A scientist helps us better understand

the ___ ___ ___ ___ ___.
    1   2   3   4   5

Scientists' Tools

These are some tools that scientists use to investigate the world. Draw a line to match the picture with the correct definition. Then write the word on the line.

| telescope | net | balance | microscope |

a tool used to gather an animal to study

_____

a tool used to make objects in the sky look larger

_____

a tool that makes small objects look much larger

_____

a tool used to measure the amount of matter an object contains

_____

Science and Engineering

Using Science Tools: A Magnifying Glass

Use a magnifying glass to look at things closely and write and draw pictures about what you see!

What You Need

- a magnifying glass
- an outdoor space

Information:
A magnifying glass, or hand lens, is a tool that scientists use to see something more clearly.

What You Do

1. Use a magnifying glass to observe the things listed below and on the next page. Write and draw about what you saw.

2. Use the example below to help you think like a scientist.

a leaf

Where I saw it: **under the tree**

What it looks like: **It is orange and has brown veins.**

How it moves/What made it move: **The wind blew the leaf off the tree.**

Draw It

an insect

Where I saw it:

_____

What it looks like:

_____

How it moves:

_____

What it was doing:

_____

Draw It

a blade of grass

Where I saw it:

_____

What it looks like:

_____

How it moves/What made it move:

_____

Draw It

Skill:

Write informational text

Engineering and Design

Pretend that you are a scientist. Tell what kind of scientist you are and write about what you are studying. Explain what you want to know and how it may help our world.

_____

_____

_____

_____

_____

_____

_____

Science

Science and Engineering   Skill Sharpeners—Science • EMC 5322 • © Evan-Moor Corp.

Engineers

Look at the picture. Read the word.
Write the word in the sentence.

design

Here is a _____,
or plan, of a bridge.

engineer

An _____ plans the
design of something.

scientist

An engineer works with a
_____ to find the
best solution.

builder

A _____ uses the
right materials for the job.

Sergei Butorin / Shutterstock.com

Engineering

Engineering

Engineers

Look all around, and you will see things that people have built. These things are useful. Before these things can be built, they need to be **designed**, or planned out. A person who designs things is called an **engineer**. An engineer must understand how the parts of something work together. In other words, he or she must know how systems work.

▲ This is the Golden Gate Bridge in San Francisco, California. The chief engineer of this bridge faced many problems during the planning. The Golden Gate is one of the longest and tallest bridges in the world, so building it was quite a task!

Some bridges have a simple design. ▼

An engineer asks questions in order to create a good system. Here are some things engineers think about before designing a project:

- How much money can we spend?

- When does it need to be done?

- What materials can we use?

- If it breaks, can we fix it easily?

To answer these questions, an engineer works with other people, such as **scientists**, **builders**, and business people. Together, they figure out the system that works best.

Word Play

Read the clue. Write the word.

1. To plan out

   ___ ___ ___ ___ ___
      4

2. A person who designs things

   ___ ___ ___ ___ ___ ___ ___ ___
         2

3. Parts of things working together

   ___ ___ ___ ___ ___ ___
         3

4. A person who knows about science

   ___ ___ ___ ___ ___ ___ ___ ___
         1

Write the numbered letters to solve the puzzle.

Science Puzzle

An engineer needs to think about money and ___ ___ ___ ___.
          1 2 3 4

    Skill Sharpeners—Science • EMC 5322 • © Evan-Moor Corp.

Engineering

Good Design

These are some things that engineers design. Draw a line to match the picture with the correct sentence. Then write the word on the line.

| light | car | bridge | fireplace |

It takes you on the road.

_____

It lets you see in the dark.

_____

It heats a home.

_____

It lets people pass over water.

_____

Engineering

Strong Garage

To find the best design, engineers make models of their projects. Design a strong garage and a weak garage using different materials.

What You Need

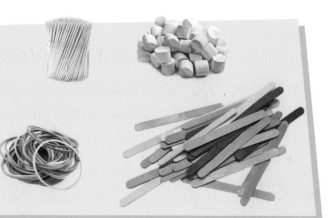

- toothpicks
- mini marshmallows
- craft sticks
- rubber bands

What You Do

1. Use the materials to make models of two different garages. Make one garage that you think will be strong and will stand by itself. A toy car should fit inside the garage.

2. Make a second garage that you think will be weak and might fall down. A toy car should also fit inside this garage.

3. Watch both garages until the weak one falls over.

Write about your designs on the Garage Record Sheet on the next page.

Garage Record Sheet

1. What materials did you use for your strong garage?

   _____

   _____

2. What materials did you use for your weak garage?

   _____

   _____

3. My strong garage has… _____ square shapes

   _____ rectangle shapes

   _____ triangle shapes

4. My weak garage has… _____ square shapes

   _____ rectangle shapes

   _____ triangle shapes

5. What made the design of the strong garage better than the design of the weak garage?

   _____

   _____

   _____

Engineering

Skill:

Write questions to demonstrate understanding of a science concept

Engineering and Design

Pretend that you are an engineer. Write four questions that you might ask yourself when designing a project.

Engineering

Answer Key

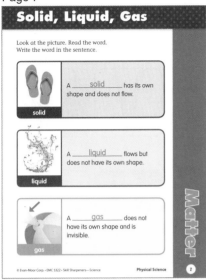

Solid, Liquid, Gas

Look at the picture. Read the word.
Write the word in the sentence.

A ___solid___ has its own shape and does not flow.

solid

A ___liquid___ flows but does not have its own shape.

liquid

A ___gas___ does not have its own shape and is invisible.

gas

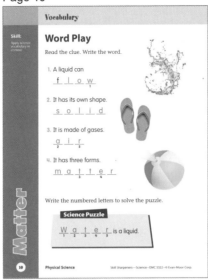

Vocabulary

Word Play

Read the clue. Write the word.

1. A liquid can
   f l o w
   1

2. It has its own shape.
   s o l i d

3. It is made of gases.
   a i r
   2   5

4. It has three forms.
   m a t t e r
   3   4

Write the numbered letters to solve the puzzle.

Science Puzzle

W a t e r is a liquid.
1 2 3 4 5

Visual Literacy

Sorting Matter Chart

Write each word in the chart.

milk   rock   water   air   toy

solid	liquid	gas
rock	water	air
toy	milk	

Three Balloons, continued

Write what happened when you tossed the balloons.

What Happened?

Frozen

How did it feel? cold

What happened when I tossed it?
It did not break.

Liquid

How did it feel? squishy

What happened when I tossed it?
It broke.

Gas

How did it feel? soft

What happened when I tossed it?
It floated to the ground.

What I Learned

Matter Chart

Solids, liquids, and gases are kinds of matter.
Complete the chart to show how they are alike or different.

Matter	Does it have its own shape?	Can you see it?	Write one example.
solid	yes	yes	sandals toy car
liquid	no	yes	water milk
gas	no	no	air

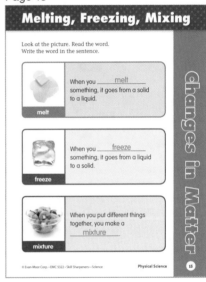

Melting, Freezing, Mixing

Look at the picture. Read the word.
Write the word in the sentence.

When you ___melt___ something, it goes from a solid to a liquid.

melt

When you ___freeze___ something, it goes from a liquid to a solid.

freeze

When you put different things together, you make a ___mixture___

mixture

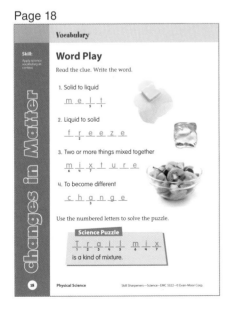

Vocabulary

Word Play

Read the clue. Write the word.

1. Solid to liquid
   m e l t
   5   1

2. Liquid to solid
   f r e e z e
   2

3. Two or more things mixed together
   m i x t u r e
   6 4   7

4. To become different
   c h a n g e
   3

Use the numbered letters to solve the puzzle.

Science Puzzle

T r a i l   m i x
1 2 3   6 4 7
is a kind of mixture.

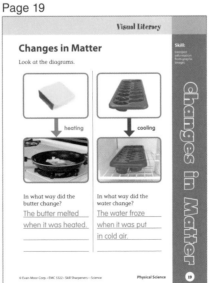

Visual Literacy

Changes in Matter

Look at the diagrams.

heating   cooling

In what way did the butter change?
The butter melted when it was heated.

In what way did the water change?
The water froze when it was put in cold air.

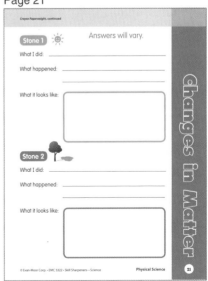

Crayon Papenweight, continued

Stone 1   Answers will vary.

What I did:

What happened:

What it looks like:

Stone 2

What I did:

What happened:

What it looks like:

Page 22

Skill: Write sentences to demonstrate understanding of science concepts

Changes Chart

Write a sentence about each picture.

Answers will vary—Examples:

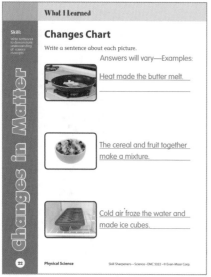

Heat made the butter melt.

The cereal and fruit together make a mixture.

Cold air froze the water and made ice cubes.

Changes in Matter

22   Physical Science   Skill Sharpeners—Science • EMC 5322 • © Evan-Moor Corp.

Page 23

Force Makes Things Move

Look at the picture. Read the word.
Write the word in the sentence.

push — When you ___push___ something, you move it away from you.

pull — When you ___pull___ something, you bring it closer to you.

force — A ___force___ is something that makes an object move.

Forces and Motion

© Evan-Moor Corp. • EMC 5322 • Skill Sharpeners—Science   Physical Science   23

Page 26

Skill: Interpret information from graphic images

What Kind of Force?

Look at the picture. What kind of force is it?
Write either **pull** or **push**.

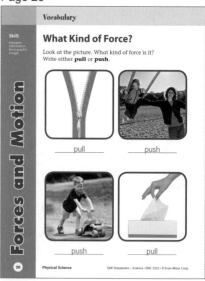

pull   push

push   pull

Forces and Motion

26   Physical Science   Skill Sharpeners—Science • EMC 5322 • © Evan-Moor Corp.

Page 27

Push, Pull, or Both?

Read the diagram.

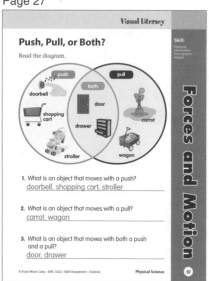

Skill: Interpret information from graphic images

1. What is an object that moves with a push?
   doorbell, shopping cart, stroller

2. What is an object that moves with a pull?
   carrot, wagon

3. What is an object that moves with both a push and a pull?
   door, drawer

Forces and Motion

© Evan-Moor Corp. • EMC 5322 • Skill Sharpeners—Science   Physical Science   27

Page 29

The Force of a Push or Pull, continued

Answers will vary.

Item	Pushed or Pulled	What happened? Did you have to use a lot of force?
toy	pushed	The toy moved. The toy was easy to push; I did not have to use a lot of force.
chair		
book		
pan		
wagon		
paper clip		

Forces and Motion

© Evan-Moor Corp. • EMC 5322 • Skill Sharpeners—Science   Physical Science   29

Page 30

Skill: Write sentences to demonstrate understanding of science concepts

How Much Force?

Write a sentence about each picture.

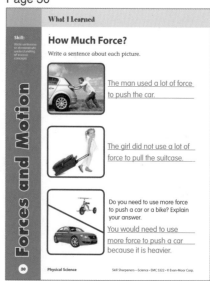

The man used a lot of force to push the car.

The girl did not use a lot of force to pull the suitcase.

Do you need to use more force to push a car or a bike? Explain your answer.
You would need to use more force to push a car because it is heavier.

Forces and Motion

30   Physical Science   Skill Sharpeners—Science • EMC 5322 • © Evan-Moor Corp.

Page 31

Magnets

Look at the picture. Read the word.
Write the word in the sentence.

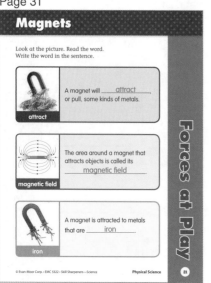

attract — A magnet will ___attract___ or pull, some kinds of metals.

magnetic field — The area around a magnet that attracts objects is called its ___magnetic field___

iron — A magnet is attracted to metals that are ___iron___.

Forces at Play

© Evan-Moor Corp. • EMC 5322 • Skill Sharpeners—Science   Physical Science   31

Page 34

Skill: Apply vocabulary in context

Word Play

Read the clue. Write the word.

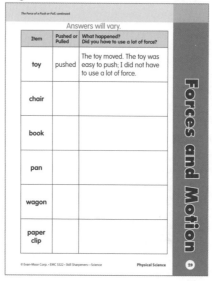

1. A kind of metal that is attracted to a magnet
   i r o n
   4 1 8

2. To pull in toward itself
   a t t r a c t
   7

3. The area around a magnet that pulls in objects
   m a g n e t i c   f i e l d
   6 5   3 2

Use the numbered letters to solve the puzzle.

Science Puzzle
People put magnets on this item made of steel.
r e f r i g e r a t o r
1 2 3 4 5 6 7 2 1 6 7 8

Forces at Play

34   Physical Science   Skill Sharpeners—Science • EMC 5322 • © Evan-Moor Corp.

Page 35

Magnetic Sentences

Mark the sentence that goes with the picture.

Skill: Interpret information from graphic images

☐ Magnets are different sizes.

☐ Magnets can attract metal through paper.

☑ Magnets attract metals that contain iron.

☐ Magnets are inside computers.

Forces at Play

© Evan-Moor Corp. • EMC 5322 • Skill Sharpeners—Science   Physical Science   35

Page 37

The Force Moves Through, continued

Object	Does the magnet stick through the object?
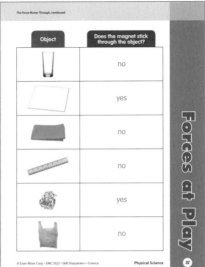	no
	yes
	no
	no
	yes
	no

Forces at Play

© Evan-Moor Corp. • EMC 5322 • Skill Sharpeners—Science   Physical Science   37

Page 38

What I Learned

Skill:

What Will Stick?

What things will a magnet attract?
Answer with words or drawings.

a nail   a metal door   a paper clip   a hammer   a car

Finish the sentence.

A magnet will attract _____ some metals

Forces at Play

38   Physical Science   Skill Sharpeners—Science • EMC 5322 • © Evan-Moor Corp.

Page 39

Grow and Change

Look at the picture. Read the word.
Write the word in the sentence.

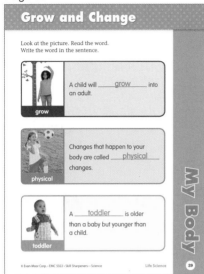

A child will ____grow____ into an adult.

grow

Changes that happen to your body are called ____physical____ changes.

physical

A ____toddler____ is older than a baby but younger than a child.

toddler

My Body

© Evan-Moor Corp. • EMC 5322 • Skill Sharpeners—Science   Life Science   39

Page 42

Vocabulary

Skill:

Then and Now

Write a word to go with the picture. Then draw a line to match then and now.

crawl   eat   talk   jump   drink   cry

Then   **Now**

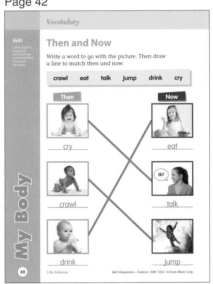

cry   eat

crawl   talk

drink   jump

My Body

42   Life Science   Skill Sharpeners—Science • EMC 5322 • © Evan-Moor Corp

Page 43

Visual Literacy

Moving Along

Write 1, 2, 3, 4, to order the pictures.

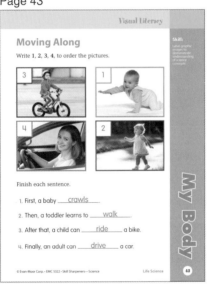

Finish each sentence.

1. First, a baby ____crawls____.
2. Then, a toddler learns to ____walk____.
3. After that, a child can ____ride____ a bike.
4. Finally, an adult can ____drive____ a car.

Skill:

My Body

© Evan-Moor Corp. • EMC 5322 • Skill Sharpeners—Science   Life Science   43

Page 44

Hands-on Activity

Skill:

Create a Timeline

Using photos or drawings, make a timeline that shows you as a baby, a toddler, and a child. Include your age, and write a caption saying what you could do at each age.

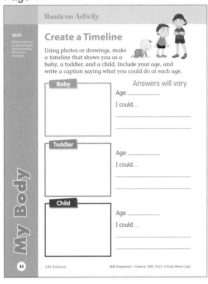

Baby

Answers will vary.

Age _____
I could…

Toddler

Age _____
I could…

Child

Age _____
I could…

My Body

44   Life Science   Skill Sharpeners—Science • EMC 5322 • © Evan-Moor Corp.

Page 45

Hands-on Activity

Hand in Hand

Make a colorful handprint picture with an adult!

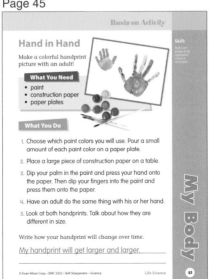

Skill:

What You Need
- paint
- construction paper
- paper plates

What You Do

1. Choose which paint colors you will use. Pour a small amount of each paint color on a paper plate.
2. Place a large piece of construction paper on a table.
3. Dip your palm in the paint and press your hand onto the paper. Then dip your fingers into the paint and press them onto the paper.
4. Have an adult do the same thing with his or her hand.
5. Look at both handprints. Talk about how they are different in size.

Write how your handprint will change over time.

My handprint will get larger and larger.

My Body

© Evan-Moor Corp. • EMC 5322 • Skill Sharpeners—Science   Life Science   45

Page 46

What I Learned

Skill:

Growth and Change Chart

Have you gotten taller? Do you weigh more? Have you learned to do something you couldn't do last year?

Complete the chart to answer these questions. Ask a parent or guardian for help if you can't remember.

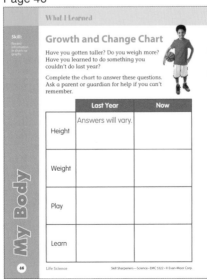

	Last Year	Now
Height	Answers will vary.	
Weight		
Play		
Learn		

My Body

46   Life Science   Skill Sharpeners—Science • EMC 5322 • © Evan-Moor Corp.

Page 47

Bones and Joints

Look at the picture. Read the word.
Write the word in the sentence.

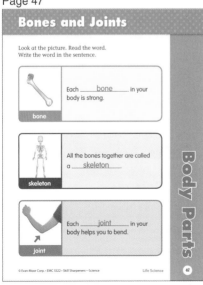

Each ____bone____ in your body is strong.

bone

All the bones together are called a ____skeleton____.

skeleton

Each ____joint____ in your body helps you to bend.

joint

Body Parts

© Evan-Moor Corp. • EMC 5322 • Skill Sharpeners—Science   Life Science   47

Vocabulary

Skill: Apply science vocabulary in context

Word Play

Read the clue. Write the word.

1. You will have 206 of these when you grow up.
   b o n e s

2. All the bones in your body make up your
   s k e l e t o n

3. These help you twist.
   j o i n t s

Write the numbered letters to solve the puzzle.

Science Puzzle

Bones and joints help you
s t a n d up and move.

Body Parts

50 Life Science Skill Sharpeners—Science • EMC 5322 • © Evan-Moor Corp.

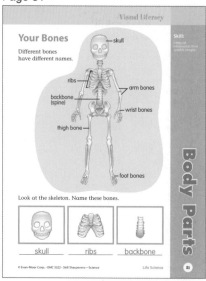

Visual Literacy

Your Bones

Different bones have different names.

- skull
- ribs
- arm bones
- backbone (spine)
- wrist bones
- thigh bone
- foot bones

Skill: Interpret information from graphic images

Look at the skeleton. Name these bones.

skull   ribs   backbone

Body Parts

© Evan-Moor Corp. • EMC 5322 • Skill Sharpeners—Science Life Science 51

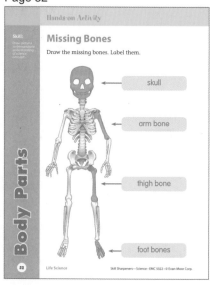

Hands-on Activity

Skill: Draw pictures to demonstrate understanding of science concept

Missing Bones

Draw the missing bones. Label them.

- skull
- arm bone
- thigh bone
- foot bones

Body Parts

52 Life Science Skill Sharpeners—Science • EMC 5322 • © Evan-Moor Corp.

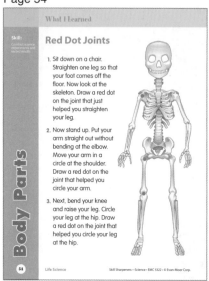

What I Learned

Skill: Conduct science experiments to produce tested results

Red Dot Joints

1. Sit down on a chair. Straighten one leg so that your foot comes off the floor. Now look at the skeleton. Draw a red dot on the joint that just helped you straighten your leg.

2. Now stand up. Put your arm straight out without bending at the elbow. Move your arm in a circle at the shoulder. Draw a red dot on the joint that helped you circle your arm.

3. Next, bend your knee and raise your leg. Circle your leg at the hip. Draw a red dot on the joint that helped you circle your leg at the hip.

Body Parts

54 Life Science Skill Sharpeners—Science • EMC 5322 • © Evan-Moor Corp.

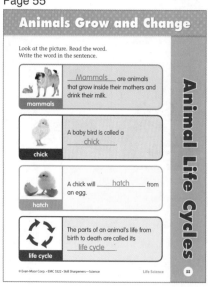

Animals Grow and Change

Look at the picture. Read the word. Write the word in the sentence.

mammals — _Mammals_ are animals that grow inside their mothers and drink their milk.

chick — A baby bird is called a _chick_.

hatch — A chick will _hatch_ from an egg.

life cycle — The parts of an animal's life from birth to death are called its _life cycle_.

Animal Life Cycles

© Evan-Moor Corp. • EMC 5322 • Skill Sharpeners—Science Life Science 55

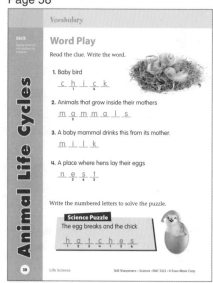

Vocabulary

Skill: Apply science vocabulary in context

Word Play

Read the clue. Write the word.

1. Baby bird
   c h i c k

2. Animals that grow inside their mothers
   m a m m a l s

3. A baby mammal drinks this from its mother.
   m i l k

4. A place where hens lay their eggs
   n e s t

Write the numbered letters to solve the puzzle.

Science Puzzle

The egg breaks and the chick
h a t c h e s

Animal Life Cycles

58 Life Science Skill Sharpeners—Science • EMC 5322 • © Evan-Moor Corp.

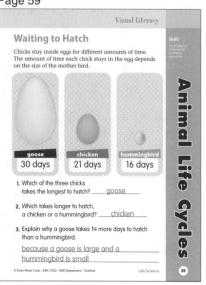

Visual Literacy

Waiting to Hatch

Chicks stay inside eggs for different amounts of time. The amount of time each chick stays in the egg depends on the size of the mother bird.

goose — 30 days
chicken — 21 days
hummingbird — 16 days

1. Which of the three chicks takes the longest to hatch? _goose_

2. Which takes longer to hatch, a chicken or a hummingbird? _chicken_

3. Explain why a goose takes 14 more days to hatch than a hummingbird.
   because a goose is large and a hummingbird is small

Animal Life Cycles

© Evan-Moor Corp. • EMC 5322 • Skill Sharpeners—Science Life Science 59

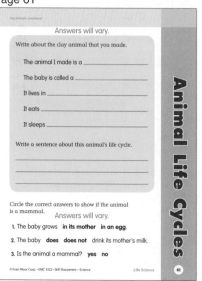

Clay Animals, continued

Answers will vary.

Write about the clay animal that you made.

The animal I made is a _____

The baby is called a _____

It lives in _____

It eats _____

It sleeps _____

Write a sentence about this animal's life cycle.

_____
_____

Circle the correct answers to show if the animal is a mammal.   Answers will vary.

1. The baby grows **in its mother** in an egg.

2. The baby **does** does not drink its mother's milk.

3. Is the animal a mammal? **yes** no

Animal Life Cycles

© Evan-Moor Corp. • EMC 5322 • Skill Sharpeners—Science Life Science 61

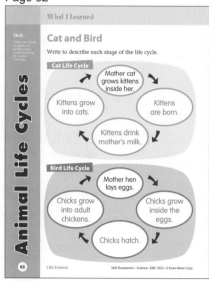

What I Learned

Skill: Carry out tasks to attach to demonstrate understanding of scientific concepts

Cat and Bird

Write to describe each stage of the life cycle.

Cat Life Cycle

- Mother cat grows kittens inside her.
- Kittens are born.
- Kittens drink mother's milk.
- Kittens grow into cats.

Bird Life Cycle

- Mother hen lays eggs.
- Chicks grow inside the eggs.
- Chicks hatch.
- Chicks grow into adult chickens.

Animal Life Cycles

62 Life Science Skill Sharpeners—Science • EMC 5322 • © Evan-Moor Corp.

Page 63

Plants Grow and Change

Look at the picture. Read the word.
Write the word in the sentence.

The ___roots___ grow into the ground.

roots

The ___stem___ is the part that connects the roots and the leaves.

stem

A ___shoot___ grows up out of the soil.

shoot

A ___pod___ holds many seeds.

pod

Page 66

Skill: Apply science vocabulary in context

Word Play

Read the clue. Write the word.

1. A plant starts with a __s e e d__

2. When the stem grows longer, these grow on the plant.
   __l e a v e s__

3. Where seeds are planted
   __s o i l__

4. The part of the plant that grows down into the ground
   __r o o t__

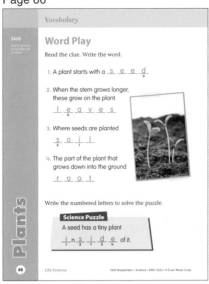

Write the numbered letters to solve the puzzle.

Science Puzzle

A seed has a tiny plant
__i n s i d e__ of it.

Page 67

Pumpkin Life Cycle

Look at each picture below. Then write the letter of the sentence that matches that picture.

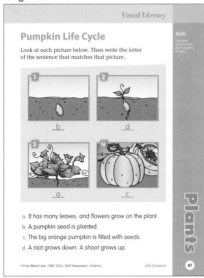

1. __b__   2. __d__
3. __a__   4. __c__

a. It has many leaves, and flowers grow on the plant.
b. A pumpkin seed is planted.
c. The big orange pumpkin is filled with seeds.
d. A root grows down. A shoot grows up.

Skill: Interpret information from graphic images.

Page 69

Life Cycle of a Pea, continued

Fill in the chart.   Answers will vary.

Week	How tall?	How many flowers?	How many seed pods?
Week 1			
Week 2			
Week 3			
Week 4			
Week 5			
Week 6			
Week 7			
Week 8			

Page 70

Skill: Write sentences to demonstrate understanding of science concepts

Pea Plant Life Cycle

Label the picture of the plant life cycle.

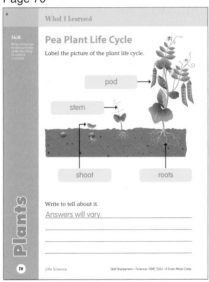

pod

stem

shoot

roots

Write to tell about it.

__Answers will vary.__

Page 71

Ocean and Desert

Look at the picture. Read the word.
Write the word in the sentence.

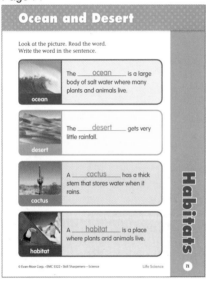

The ___ocean___ is a large body of salt water where many plants and animals live.

ocean

The ___desert___ gets very little rainfall.

desert

A ___cactus___ has a thick stem that stores water when it rains.

cactus

A ___habitat___ is a place where plants and animals live.

habitat

Page 74

Skill: Apply science vocabulary in context

Word Play

Read the clue. Write the word.

1. Some desert animals come out only at __n i g h t__

2. The wettest habitat is the __o c e a n__

3. The driest habitat is the __d e s e r t__

4. The __c a c t u s__ is a desert __p l a n t__ that stores water in its stem.

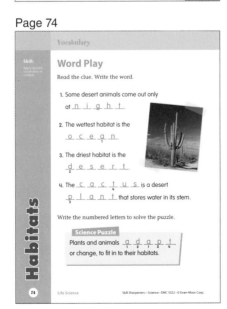

Write the numbered letters to solve the puzzle.

Science Puzzle

Plants and animals __a d a p t__ or change, to fit in to their habitats.

Page 75

Compare the Ocean and Desert

Read the diagram.

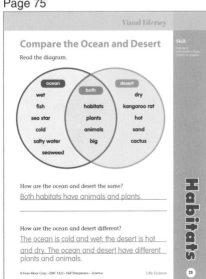

ocean: wet, fish, sea star, cold, salty water, seaweed
both: habitats, plants, animals, big
desert: dry, kangaroo rat, hot, sand, cactus

Skill: Interpret information from charts or graphs

How are the ocean and desert the same?
__Both habitats have animals and plants.__

How are the ocean and desert different?
__The ocean is cold and wet; the desert is hot and dry. The ocean and desert have different plants and animals.__

Page 78

Skill: Complete charts or graphs to demonstrate understanding of science concepts

Ocean and Desert Life

Write the names of plants and animals that you can find in the ocean and the desert.

fish	seaweed	cactus
kangaroo rat	lizard	sea star

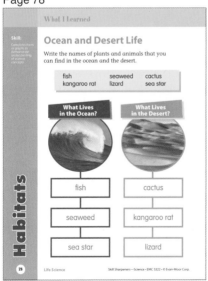

What Lives in the Ocean?

fish

seaweed

sea star

What Lives in the Desert?

cactus

kangaroo rat

lizard

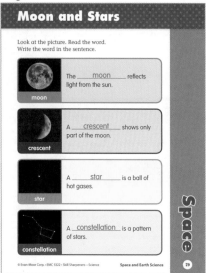

Moon and Stars

Look at the picture. Read the word.
Write the word in the sentence.

moon — The __moon__ reflects light from the sun.

crescent — A __crescent__ shows only part of the moon.

star — A __star__ is a ball of hot gases.

constellation — A __constellation__ is a pattern of stars.

Space

Vocabulary

Skill: Apply science vocabulary in context

Word Play

Read the clue. Write the word.

1. Big, round moon
   f u l l m o o n

2. Look like tiny dots of light
   s t a r s

3. The planet you are on
   E a r t h

4. The moon when it is shaped like a banana
   c r e s c e n t m o o n

Write the numbered letters to solve the puzzle.

Science Puzzle
The Big Dipper is a
c o n s t e l l a t i o n

Space

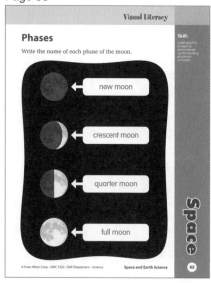

Visual Literacy

Phases

Write the name of each phase of the moon.

- new moon
- crescent moon
- quarter moon
- full moon

Skill: Label graphic images to demonstrate understanding of science concepts.

Space

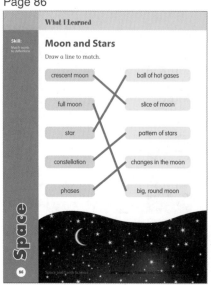

What I Learned

Skill: Match words to definitions

Moon and Stars

Draw a line to match.

crescent moon — slice of moon
full moon — big, round moon
star — ball of hot gases
constellation — pattern of stars
phases — changes in the moon

Space

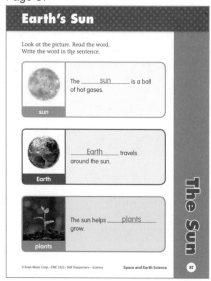

Earth's Sun

Look at the picture. Read the word.
Write the word in the sentence.

sun — The __sun__ is a ball of hot gases.

Earth — __Earth__ travels around the sun.

plants — The sun helps __plants__ grow.

The Sun

Vocabulary

Skill: Apply science vocabulary in context

Word Play

Read the clue. Write the word.

1. The star closest to Earth
   s u n

2. The sun gives off this so you can see.
   l i g h t

3. The time it takes for Earth to travel all the way around the sun
   y e a r

4. The sun gives us this to stay warm.
   h e a t

Write the numbered letters to solve the puzzle.

Science Puzzle
We cannot see the sun at
n i g h t

The Sun

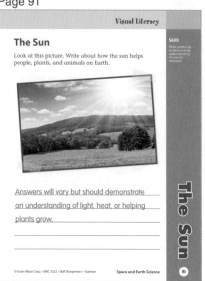

Visual Literacy

The Sun

Look at this picture. Write about how the sun helps people, plants, and animals on Earth.

Skill: Write sentences to demonstrate understanding of science concepts

Answers will vary but should demonstrate an understanding of light, heat, or helping plants grow.

The Sun

Hands-on Activity

Skill: Conduct experiments and record results

Sun Picture

See how the light from the sun can cause changes.

What You Need
- tape
- foam stickers or shapes
- dark construction paper

What You Do

1. Arrange the shapes on the construction paper.

2. Tape the construction paper to a sunny window, facing out.

3. After a week, take down the construction paper and remove the shapes. Look at the construction paper and answer the question.

What did the sun do to the construction paper?
The sun faded the construction paper except for where the shapes had been.

The Sun

What I Learned

Skill: Write sentences to demonstrate understanding of science concepts

Sun Facts

Write to tell what you learned about the sun.

What is the sun?
The sun is a ball of hot gases. It is the closest star to Earth.

Why does the sun look small?
The sun looks small because it is so far away.

How does the sun help people, plants, and animals?
The sun gives Earth heat and light. People, plants, and animals need the sun's light to live.

The Sun

Page 95

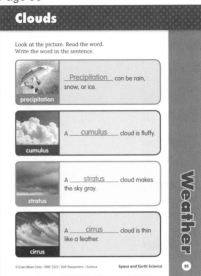

Clouds

Look at the picture. Read the word.
Write the word in the sentence.

Precipitation can be rain, snow, or ice.

precipitation

A _cumulus_ cloud is fluffy.

cumulus

A _stratus_ cloud makes the sky gray.

stratus

A _cirrus_ cloud is thin like a feather.

cirrus

Weather

Page 98

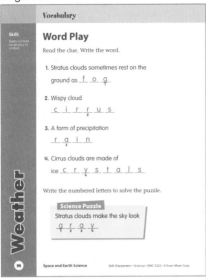

Vocabulary

Skill: Apply content vocabulary in context

Word Play

Read the clue. Write the word.

1. Stratus clouds sometimes rest on the ground as f o g

2. Wispy cloud
   c i r r u s

3. A form of precipitation
   r a i n

4. Cirrus clouds are made of
   ice c r y s t a l s

Write the numbered letters to solve the puzzle.

Science Puzzle
Stratus clouds make the sky look
g r a y

Weather

Page 99

Visual Literacy

Skill: Label graphic images to demonstrate understanding of science concepts

Cloud Names

Write the name of each cloud.

cirrus   stratus   cumulus

cumulus

stratus

cirrus

Weather

Page 100

Hands-on Activity

Skill: Conduct experiments and answer questions

Cloud in a Glass

Make a cumulus cloud in a glass and then make it rain.

What You Need
- shaving cream
- clear glass
- water   • blue food coloring

What You Do

1. Fill the glass halfway with water.

2. Pile a mound of shaving cream on top of the water in the glass. Make it look like a fluffy cumulus cloud.

3. Drip some blue food coloring onto the cumulus cloud. Watch as the cloud absorbs the water. Soon, the cloud will get too heavy and blue drops will fall from the cloud.

How is this similar to how rain really happens?
Answers will vary.

Weather

Page 102

What I Learned

Skill: Label graphic images to demonstrate understanding of science concepts

Word Cloud

Next to each picture, write the name of the cloud you learned about. Then write two words to describe each cloud.

cumulus
fluffy
pile

stratus
gray
layer

cirrus
feather
curl

Weather

Page 103

Land Changes

Look at the picture. Read the word.
Write the word in the sentence.

Erosion carries away rock and soil.

erosion

Weathering breaks down or wears away rock.

weathering

People also shape the _surface_ of the land.

surface

Geology

Page 106

Vocabulary

Skill: Apply science vocabulary in context

Word Play

Read the clue. Write the word.

1. This part of Earth changes over time.
   s u r f a c e

2. This carries rock and soil away.
   e r o s i o n

3. The wearing away of rock is called
   w e a t h e r i n g

4. Nature doesn't stay the same; it
   c h a n g e s

Write the numbered letters to solve the puzzle.

Science Puzzle
The land is changed by different
f o r c e s

Geology

Page 107

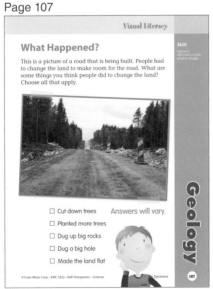

Visual Literacy

Skill: Interpret information from graphic images

What Happened?

This is a picture of a road that is being built. People had to change the land to make room for the road. What are some things you think people did to change the land? Choose all that apply.

Answers will vary.

☐ Cut down trees
☐ Planted more trees
☐ Dug up big rocks
☐ Dug a big hole
☐ Made the land flat

Geology

Page 108

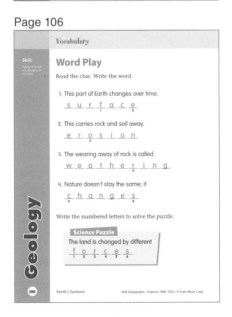

Hands-on Activity

Skill: Conduct experiments and answer questions

Weathering Rocks

Rocks in a stream become weathered when they are tumbled by the water. Here is how you can weather rocks yourself.

What You Need
- handful of gravel
- 2 small jars with tight lids
- 2 coffee filters
- strainer
- bowl
- water

What You Do

1. Place half the gravel in each jar, and fill the jars with water.

2. Shake one jar as many times as you can in 2 minutes. Do not shake the other jar.

3. Place a coffee filter inside the strainer. Hold it over the bowl. Pour everything from the jar you shook into the filter. Let the water drain.

4. Take the rocks out of the filter, but leave the sand. Then lay the sandy filter flat to dry.

5. Repeat Steps 3 and 4 with the unshaken jar.

Why did one filter have more sand?
The first jar had more sand because I shook
it a lot and the water weathered the rocks.

Geology

Page 109

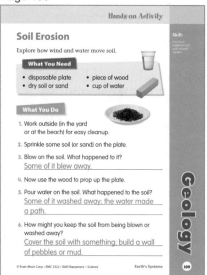

Soil Erosion

Explore how wind and water move soil.

What You Need
- disposable plate
- dry soil or sand
- piece of wood
- cup of water

What You Do

1. Work outside (in the yard or at the beach) for easy cleanup.
2. Sprinkle some soil (or sand) on the plate.
3. Blow on the soil. What happened to it?
   Some of it blew away.
4. Now use the wood to prop up the plate.
5. Pour water on the soil. What happened to the soil?
   Some of it washed away; the water made a path.
6. How might you keep the soil from being blown or washed away?
   Cover the soil with something; build a wall of pebbles or mud.

Skill: Conduct experiments and record results

Geology

© Evan-Moor Corp. • EMC 5322 • Skill Sharpeners—Science   Earth's Systems   109

Page 110

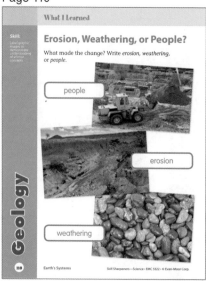

Erosion, Weathering, or People?

What made the change? Write *erosion*, *weathering*, or *people*.

people

erosion

weathering

Skill: Label graphic images to demonstrate understanding of science concepts

Geology

110   Earth's Systems   Skill Sharpeners—Science • EMC 5322 • © Evan-Moor Corp.

Page 111

Water on Earth

Look at the picture. Read the word.
Write the word in the sentence.

salt water — Most of Earth's water is salt water.

glacier — A glacier is made of frozen fresh water.

fresh water — Fresh water is the water we can drink.

iceberg — An iceberg is ice that floats in the ocean.

Water and Ice

© Evan-Moor Corp. • EMC 5322 • Skill Sharpeners—Science   Earth's Systems   111

Page 114

Word Play

Skill: Apply science vocabulary in context

Read the clue. Write the word.

1. Water in the ocean
   s a l t   w a t e r
       4   3

2. A sheet of ice on land
   g l a c i e r
           1

3. Ice floating in the ocean
   i c e b e r g
         2

4. Water you can drink
   f r e s h   w a t e r
           5   6

Write the numbered letters to solve the puzzle.

Science Puzzle
A very large glacier is called an
i c e   s h e e t
1 2 3   4 5 6 7

Water and Ice

114   Earth's Systems   Skill Sharpeners—Science • EMC 5322 • © Evan-Moor Corp.

Page 115

Water and Ice

Write the name of each type of Earth's water.

glacier   iceberg   fresh water   salt water

salt water   iceberg

fresh water   glacier

Skill: Label graphic images to demonstrate understanding of science concepts

Water and Ice

© Evan-Moor Corp. • EMC 5322 • Skill Sharpeners—Science   Earth's Systems   115

Page 118

Types of Water and Ice

In the boxes below, write the names of the two types of water and ice you learned about, and describe them.

Skill: Write sentences to demonstrate understanding of science concepts

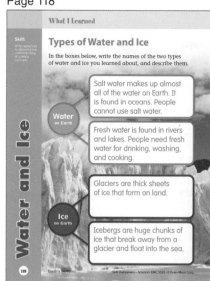

Water on Earth

Salt water makes up almost all of the water on Earth. It is found in oceans. People cannot use salt water.

Fresh water is found in rivers and lakes. People need fresh water for drinking, washing, and cooking.

Ice on Earth

Glaciers are thick sheets of ice that form on land.

Icebergs are huge chunks of ice that break away from a glacier and float into the sea.

Water and Ice

118   Earth's Systems   Skill Sharpeners—Science • EMC 5322 • © Evan-Moor Corp.

Page 119

Scientists

Look at the picture. Read the word.
Write the word in the sentence.

scientist — A scientist studies the world to find out how it works.

botanist — A botanist is a scientist who studies plants.

zoologist — A zoologist is a scientist who studies animals.

meteorologist — A meteorologist is a scientist who studies weather.

Science

© Evan-Moor Corp. • EMC 5322 • Skill Sharpeners—Science   Science and Engineering   119

Page 122

Word Play

Skill: Apply science vocabulary in context

Read the clue. Write the word.

1. A scientist who studies animals
   z o o l o g i s t

2. What a meteorologist studies
   w e a t h e r

3. Scientists conduct these.
   e x p e r i m e n t s

4. Scientists solve these problems.
   r e a l - l i f e

5. Scientists make these by doing experiments.
   d i s c o v e r i e s

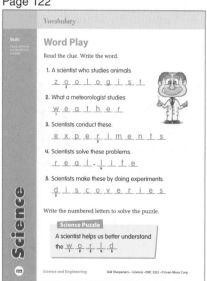

Write the numbered letters to solve the puzzle.

Science Puzzle
A scientist helps us better understand
the w o r l d
    1 2 3 4 5

Science

122   Science and Engineering   Skill Sharpeners—Science • EMC 5322 • © Evan-Moor Corp.

Page 123

Scientists' Tools

Skill: Interpret information from graphic images

These are some tools that scientists use to investigate the world. Draw a line to match the picture with the correct definition. Then write the word on the line.

telescope   net   balance   microscope

a tool used to gather an animal to study
net

a tool used to make objects in the sky look larger
microscope

a tool that makes small objects look much larger
telescope

a tool used to measure the amount of matter an object contains
balance

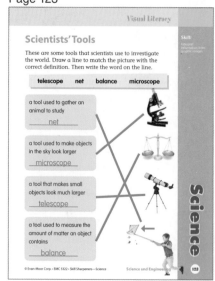

Science

© Evan-Moor Corp. • EMC 5322 • Skill Sharpeners—Science   Science and Engineering   123

Page 125

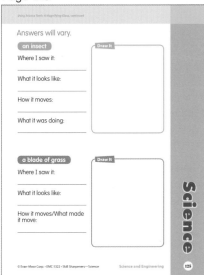

Answers will vary.

an insect

Where I saw it:

What it looks like:

How it moves:

What it was doing:

Draw It

a blade of grass

Where I saw it:

What it looks like:

How it moves/What made it move:

Draw It

© Evan-Moor Corp. • EMC 5322 • Skill Sharpeners—Science   Science and Engineering   125

Science

Page 126

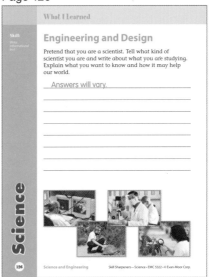

Skill:
Write informational text

What I Learned

Engineering and Design

Pretend that you are a scientist. Tell what kind of scientist you are and write about what you are studying. Explain what you want to know and how it may help our world.

_____Answers will vary._____

126   Science and Engineering   Skill Sharpeners—Science • EMC 5322 • © Evan-Moor Corp.

Science

Page 127

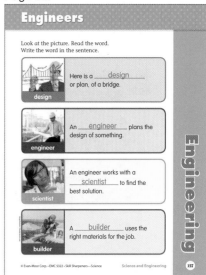

Engineers

Look at the picture. Read the word.
Write the word in the sentence.

design — Here is a ___design___, or plan, of a bridge.

engineer — An ___engineer___ plans the design of something.

scientist — An engineer works with a ___scientist___ to find the best solution.

builder — A ___builder___ uses the right materials for the job.

© Evan-Moor Corp. • EMC 5322 • Skill Sharpeners—Science   Science and Engineering   127

Engineering

Page 130

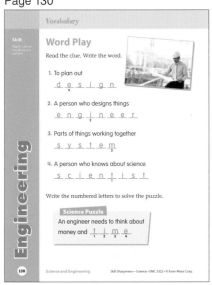

Skill:
Apply science vocabulary in context

Vocabulary

Word Play

Read the clue. Write the word.

1. To plan out
   d e s i g n
         4

2. A person who designs things
   e n g i n e e r
       2

3. Parts of things working together
   s y s t e m
           3

4. A person who knows about science
   s c i e n t i s t
             1

Write the numbered letters to solve the puzzle.

Science Puzzle
An engineer needs to think about
money and t i m e .
          1 2 3 4

130   Science and Engineering   Skill Sharpeners—Science • EMC 5322 • © Evan-Moor Corp.

Engineering

Page 131

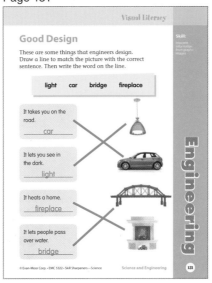

Visual Literacy

Skill:
Interpret information from graphic images

Good Design

These are some things that engineers design. Draw a line to match the picture with the correct sentence. Then write the word on the line.

| light | car | bridge | fireplace |

It takes you on the road.
___car___

It lets you see in the dark.
___light___

It heats a home.
___fireplace___

It lets people pass over water.
___bridge___

© Evan-Moor Corp. • EMC 5322 • Skill Sharpeners—Science   Science and Engineering   131

Engineering

Page 133

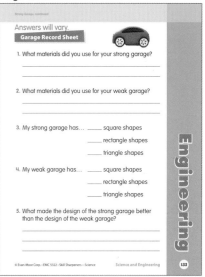

Strong Garage, continued

Answers will vary.

Garage Record Sheet

1. What materials did you use for your strong garage?

2. What materials did you use for your weak garage?

3. My strong garage has... ___ square shapes
   ___ rectangle shapes
   ___ triangle shapes

4. My weak garage has... ___ square shapes
   ___ rectangle shapes
   ___ triangle shapes

5. What made the design of the strong garage better than the design of the weak garage?

© Evan-Moor Corp. • EMC 5322 • Skill Sharpeners—Science   Science and Engineering   133

Engineering

Page 134

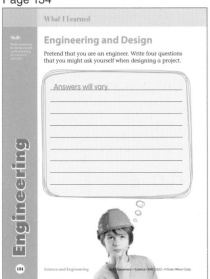

Skill:
Write questions to demonstrate understanding of a science concept

What I Learned

Engineering and Design

Pretend that you are an engineer. Write four questions that you might ask yourself when designing a project.

Answers will vary.

134   Science and Engineering   Skill Sharpeners—Science • EMC 5322 • © Evan-Moor Corp.

Engineering

Here's how parents turn "I'm bored! There's nothing to do!" into "I'm *never* bored!"

The Never-Bored Kid Books

Ages 4–9   This exciting, colorful series will engage kids in hours of productive fun. There are hidden pictures, puzzles, things to cut out and create, pop-ups, art projects, word games, and a whole lot more!   **evan-moor.com/nbkb**

The Never-Bored Kid Book

Ages 4–5	EMC 6300
Ages 5–6	EMC 6303
Ages 6–7	EMC 6301
Ages 7–8	EMC 6304
Ages 8–9	EMC 6302

160 full-color pages.

The Never-Bored Kid Book 2

Ages 4–5	EMC 6307
Ages 5–6	EMC 6308
Ages 6–7	EMC 6309
Ages 7–8	EMC 6310
Ages 8–9	EMC 6311

144 full-color pages.

*iParenting Media Hot Award Winner

Flashcards

These aren't your average flashcards! Our flashcards include an interactive component with access to online timed tests. The corresponding online activities add another dimension to flashcard practice. Each flashcard set motivates young learners to practice an important readiness concept or fundamental skill.

56 full-color flashcards

56 full-color flashcards.

AGES 4–7+

Reading

Colors and Shapes	**Ages 4+**	EMC 4161
The Alphabet	**Ages 4+**	EMC 4162
Vowel Sounds	**Ages 5+**	EMC 4163
Word Families	**Ages 6+**	EMC 4164
Sight Words	**Ages 6+**	EMC 4165

Math

Counting 1–20	**Ages 4+**	EMC 4166
Counting 1–100	**Ages 5+**	EMC 4167
Addition and Subtraction Facts to 10	**Ages 5+**	EMC 4168
Addition Facts 11–18	**Ages 6+**	EMC 4169
Subtraction Facts 11–18	**Ages 6+**	EMC 4170
Multiplication Facts to 9s	**Ages 7+**	EMC 4171
Division Facts to 9s	**Ages 7+**	EMC 4172

with online timed tests!